# Pilgrim Tips

WITHDRAWN

# &

# Packing List

## Camino de Santiago

D0972489

What you need to know beforehand, what you
need to take, and what you can leave at home.

**S. Yates** with **Daphne Hnatiuk**

**Copyright**: All rights reserved. No part of this publication, neither text nor images, may be reproduced, stored in a retrieval system, or transmitted in any form or by any means, electronic, mechanical, photocopying, recording, translating, or otherwise, without the prior, written consent of Sybille Yates. The only exception to this are short text excerpts included in an editorial review.

**Disclaimer**: This book provides information about the pilgrimage on the Camino de Santiago. It is sold with the provision that the author does not accept any responsibility regarding what the reader does with the provided information. This book's intent is to educate and to inform. Neither Sybille Yates, nor any vendor or importer, can be held liable by any person or entity, regarding any damages or losses caused directly or indirectly by this book, or are presumed to have been caused by this book, and/or are resulting from participating in the activities described in this book. The author has taken great care to present all information in this book as exact and complete as possible. Nevertheless, no warranty can be assumed for its content. Especially not for the everlasting correctness of prices, addresses, contact information such as telephone numbers, website addresses or similar.

**Imprint**

Copyright Text and Cover 2013 © Sybille Yates

Author: Sybille Yates

Co-Author & Editor: Daphne Hnatiuk

Print Edition April 2013 (version 1.0)

ISBN-13: 978-1484079843

ISBN-10: 1484079841

# Table of Contents

**Introduction**                                                    **4**
Welcome to Europe!                                                   6
Two Reasons why Pilgrims Pack Too Much Stuff                        11
And the Dogs on the Camino?                                         11
A Typical Pilgrim's Day                                            13
Different Kinds of Pilgrims                                         14
Which Route and When?                                               16
Technology and a Thousand Years Old Pilgrimage Route               23
Every Gram Counts                                                   25
**General Thoughts about the Necessary Equipment**                 **27**
Women Specific Pilgrim Tips                                         29
Men Specific Pilgrim Tips                                           30
LGBTQ Specific Pilgrim Tips                                         31
**General Tips for Weight Reduction**                              **32**
Combinations and Multi-Use Purposes of Your Gear                   32
Pilgrims with Animals                                               35
Food, Drink and Water                                              37
How Much Should Your Backpack Weigh?                                45
More Tips for Pilgrims                                              45
**Your Gear**
What Every Pilgrim Needs                                           54
Weightless Items                                                   54
What Some Pilgrims Might Need                                       98
Luxury Items                                                       105
Symbols                                                            109
What a Pilgrim, in Most Cases, Doesn't Need                       111
Packing and Carrying                                              114
**After the Way**                                                **120**
About the Authors and a Request                                   122
**Appendix**                                                     **123**

# Introduction - Why I Wrote this Book

Hundreds of thousands of people go to Spain every year to walk the Camino de Santiago to visit the tomb of St. James, one of Jesus Christ's first disciples.

Some walk only a section of the Way, some the whole Way. But around a third of them give up during their first few days and spend the rest of their vacation at the beach or at home. Why? The main reason for this is that they have not done enough preparation and are carrying far too much weight in their backpack. Each additional kilo burdens the back, the joints and the feet and makes it more probable that health problems will arise. And these health problems, unfortunately, often lead to the premature termination of their pilgrimage. As well, not bringing important items in your backpack can cause problems, for example, having no sun protection.

I will not only explain in this book what should be taken and what should be left at home, but also how to best pack your backpack so that it is easy to carry and does not become a burden. This book focuses on the pilgrimage on the main Spanish pilgrimage route, the Camino Francés, but the underlying principles can be applied to other pilgrimage routes, other long-distance walks, and even a weekend hike.

I have walked over 6,000 kilometres (3,700 miles) on European pilgrimage routes with all I needed on my back, and I have helped as a volunteer (*hospitalera*) in over 20 pilgrim *refugios* in Spain. You could say that I have "a little bit" of experience when it comes to packing - and unpacking - a pilgrim's backpack.

To avoid this book becoming too "dry" I have seasoned it with a few Pilgrim's Anecdotes. Names, nationalities, and places of origin have been altered to protect the privacy of said pilgrims. Here are three of my favourite memories of pilgrims who packed too much:

### ***Pilgrim's Anecdote***

• *The young French pilgrim Jacqueline, who had a little gas stove in her backpack, to heat the wax to depilate her legs.*

• *The not so young Brazilian pilgrim Dolores, who carried seven different sets of rain clothes - each set consisted of waterproof trousers, jacket and poncho. She had one set for every day of the week and in seven different colours.*

    • *The two young pilgrims from Canada, Pierre and Paul, who, with an aim to save money, brought their fishing rods in the hope of catching tasty trout on the Camino.*

*Difficult to say who should win!*

\*\*\*

It is not only newbie pilgrims who make mistakes when it comes to packing a backpack. During my third Camino, I packed my first parcel to be sent home after only five days. Despite the fact that I had already walked hundreds of kilometres in the past years and had helped dozens of pilgrims to de-clutter their backpacks, I had again, taken too much with me. If I remember correctly, the first time that I did not take anything superfluous with me was during my fifth Camino - Yes, I am indeed a slow learner! And because of this, I wrote this book. I hope that you can get it right from the beginning and can learn from my mistakes. This is the book that I wish had been available before I started out on my first Camino, and then I would have known not to take with me all sorts of things that I might perhaps need somewhere, under certain circumstances, and then never ever did!

## Who is this book written for?

This book is mainly written for the, statistically, largest group of pilgrims: the traditional pilgrims that carry all their luggage on their backs and walk the entire route from St Jean Pied-de-Port to Santiago de Compostela. More as to where the Camino starts, and what is "the whole Camino", a bit further down.

But that does not mean that *"bicigrinos"*, pilgrims on a bike, cannot benefit from it. But this book does not address their needs specifically. It is also meant more for pilgrims who walk the Camino de Santiago for the very first time, rather than for the "repeat offenders", but I still hope that "old pilgrim hands" find something useful in it too.

# How this book is organized

The first part gives information about the different aspects of the life of a pilgrim and the second addresses each bit of equipment that all or most pilgrims will need. With this I hope, that not only the "What" becomes clear to the reader, but also the "Why". In the end it is you that needs to make an informed decision. In all the years, both as a *hospitalera*, as well as a pilgrim, I have not yet met one single pilgrim who wished they had taken more, but plenty that wished they had taken less.

And in the third part, the appendix, you will find links to customizable documents, both pdf and doc, which you can download, edit, print, and use to make your own personalized packing list. Additionally you will find many useful addresses, useful websites, and some, hopefully, interesting texts.

**Gender note:**

In the interest of being concise and avoiding having to continually write he/she or him/her please note that throughout this book, when I write he, I always also mean she and the word 'man' refers to a 'woman' as well. Sorry sister *peregrinas*.


# Welcome to Europe!

**Camino Terms**

Writing a book in English should be easy, but the truth is, it isn't. The reason is that there are not only many different versions of English, but also the same words can mean different things in different English-speaking countries. Add to this that some of these countries use the metric system, (kilometres, grams, and kilos), whilst others use the imperial system, (yards, miles, ounces, and even stones). And the real fun starts when some Spanish words like *"refugio"* or *"hospitalera/o"* don't have an exact translation into English. To keep this book as useful as possible for as many readers from as many countries as possible, here is what we have done: We have used Canadian English! (The reason being that the editor is Canadian.)

Spanish words and expressions which are pretty much part of the everyday Camino language of pilgrims, are used in this book in the same way that they are spoken on the Camino. Below are these respective words and their explanations:

**Santiago = Saint (St.) James**: This one needs a bit of explaining. In the New Testament, which was written in Greek, Santiago is called *Iacobos,* which is the equivalent of the Hebrew name Jacob. Over time, and under the influence of Latin, this became **Sanct**us (Saint) **Iaco**bus which then was contracted and underwent an additional consonant change from "c" to "g" to become Santiago, the name nowadays used in Spain for St. James. St. James is the direct English translation of the Hebrew name "Jacob". Therefore the correct translation for Camino de Santiago is Way of St. James, but in everyday pilgrim life you mostly hear "Camino" or "The Way".

**Camino/Camino de Santiago**: Way of St. James - All Ways lead to Santiago de Compostela and this is the umbrella term for all the Camino routes.

**Santiago de Compostela**: The town in Northern Spain, in the Province of Galicia where it is said that the remains of St. James are buried and housed in the Cathedral of the Apostle. This is the destination of the pilgrimage and the town is often referred to simply as 'Santiago'.

**Camino Francés**: Literally translated 'French Way', the main pilgrimage route in Spain, starting in either Roncesvalles, Spain (Navarra province) or Somport, Spain (Aragon province) and merging in Puente la Reina. From Puente la Reina onwards, it is properly called the Camino Francés. Before that, it is respectively known as the Camino de Navarra or as the Camino Aragones.

**Compostela**: A certificate in Latin issued by the Pilgrim's Office in Santiago de Compostela, indicating that you have either walked the last 100 km or ridden a bicycle/horse the last 200 km into Santiago de Compostela on the Camino, for either religious or spiritual reasons.

**Credential**: the Pilgrim's Passport that you carry and get rubber stamps in to indicate that you are a Pilgrim on the Way.

**Sello/Stamp**: A rubber stamp (not a postage stamp!) that you collect in your *credencial*. They are issued by all *albergues* and by most hotels, bars, and restaurants along the Camino. The *hospitalero* will also write the date under the stamp and sometimes sign it as well.

**Peregrino/a** : Pilgrim. *Peregrina* is a female pilgrim, *peregrino* a male pilgrim. The plural is *peregrinos*, unless all are female, then they are *peregrinas*. Don't you just love languages that have genders?!

**Hospitalero/a (Voluntario/a)** - A volunteer that takes care of the *refugio* (see below) and the pilgrims staying in it.

**Hospitaleros Voluntarios** - Both an umbrella term for all *hospitaleros* and the proper name of the biggest Spanish volunteer organization. The closest English term is "warden", but that does have some negative connotations (prison warden) which make it, in our opinion, not really suitable to describe the work done by *Hospitaleros Voluntarios*.

**Refugio/Albergue/Hospital de Peregrinos** - The place, roughly comparable to a simple Youth Hostel, where pilgrims spend the night on the Camino. Followed by the following terms that indicate the ownership: (eg. Refugio Privado)

**Privado** - Private

**Municipal** – Public - maintained by the village, town or city

**Parroquial** - maintained by the Church or parish

**Monastico** - maintained by a monastery

The English word "refuge" captures only part of this meaning, so we decided to use the Spanish word *"refugio"* throughout this book as these places are so much more than, for example, a simple mountain hut refuge.


**Money**

Most European countries, including Spain and France, have adopted the Euro as a common currency. To get the up to date exchange rate go to http://www.xe.com/ucc/.

The conversion rates at the time of writing (April 2013):

1 Euro = 0.83 GBP = 1.33 USD = 1.27 AUD = 11.63 ZAR = 1.60 NZD = 1.31 CAD

## Metric Measurements

The Camino de Santiago is in Europe and at least in continental Europe, all measurements are metric for distance, weight, and temperature. If you come from a country that uses other measurements, it might be a good idea to familiarize yourself with the metric way of doing things as you will encounter them every day during your pilgrimage. Here is a handy summary to get you started:

## 24 hour clock

Europe uses the 24 hour clock and thus we have used it throughout this book as well. This means that the sign on the *refugio* that says *"Abierto a las 13:00"*, means it will open at 1:00 pm, and the sign on the grocery store that reads "Cerrado a las 20:30", means that it will close at 8:30 pm.

## Phone numbers

To dial from Spain to say, Canada, you dial 00 + 1 (country code for Canada) + the 10 digit number in Canada. To dial from Spain to the UK, you dial 00 + 44 (country code for the UK) followed by the UK number minus the zero at the beginning. To dial to other countries, just insert the respective country code ;-)

To dial to Spain from Canada, you dial 011 + 34 (country code for Spain) + the 9 digit Spanish number. To dial to Spain from the UK, you dial 00 + 34 + the 9 digit Spanish number.

The country code for Spain is 34 and for France is 33.

## Temperature

If someone in Spain tells you that tomorrow's expected temperature will be 25°, it means it will be a pleasant day, as this is the Celsius equivalent of 77°F.

To convert Celsius easily into Fahrenheit: °C × 1.8 + 32 = °F  To get a rough idea just multiply the temperature in Celsius x 2 and then add 32.

Here are some "orientation points" when it comes to temperatures: 0°C = 32°F, 37°C = 100°F, and 100°C = 212°F

## Distances

One mile is 1.6 kilometres long. To convert from kilometres to miles simply multiply the number of kilometres by 5 and divide by 8. To convert from miles to kilometres, multiply the number of miles by 8 and divide by 5.

Here some examples: 1 km = 0.62 mi., 5 km = 3.1 mi. and 8 km = 5 mi.

## Weight

A kilogram consists of 1000g and is the equivalent to 2.2 pounds or 35.3 oz. On the other hand one pound equals roughly 0.450 kg and one ounce equals 28g. To convert from kilograms into pounds simply divide by 2 to get a rough idea. To convert from grams into ounces you can divide by 4 to get a rough estimate. Here are two more conversions to get you started: 100g = 3.5 oz or 0.22 pounds and 500g = 17.6 oz or 1.1 pound.

## Liquid measures

Litres is what is used in Spain, and when it comes to water, you will need to drink many of those each day on the Camino! 1 litre is roughly one US Quart, or a little under two UK pints so that one is relatively easy.

# Two Reasons why Pilgrims Pack Too Much Stuff

Fear and insecurity, and the marketing that takes advantage of them, are the main reasons why pilgrims carry far too much on the Camino. The worst argument for packing something in the backpack is "just in case". This case barely ever happens, but the weight stays with you the whole way. But fear and insecurity develop not only out of lack of information, but also from false information.

Here is where marketing raises its ugly head. For a product to sell there has to a demand for it and, if there is no demand, you have to create one artificially. Two good examples of this are theft protection (PacSafe®) and dog repellent. PacSafe® is a metal net that you put over your backpack for theft protection and that

a) signals to a prospective thief that there is something valuable and worth stealing inside your backpack and

b) increases the weight of your backpack dramatically. Not recommended!

The best theft protection is to leave all valuables, such as jewellery and expensive watches, at home. And not to leave anything that is worth stealing, unsupervised or lying around. This means that all your valuables, including passport and bank cards, should always be worn on your body and even carried with you into the shower - in a waterproof bag.

# And the Dogs on the Camino?

**Important:** No matter what Shirley MacLaine, Paulo Cuelho and others write in their novels, dogs that bite or attack pilgrims are the absolute exception on the Camino, not the rule!

The dogs on the Camino fall mainly into the category of "Village and /or Working Dogs" and they will leave you in peace if you leave them in peace. Instead of arming yourself with pepper spray, whistles and ultra sound gadgets, here is a simple, free, and weightless method to repel unwanted canine attention - click your tongue! In Spain, this is a sign for dogs to go away, not to come to you as in other parts of the world.

Dogs that accompany flocks of sheep are there to protect them against theft and predators, as well as against strangers. Please take a wide berth around these cute, white, woolly-fluffy clouds and their canine guardians.

A word of caution when it comes to pepper sprays and similar; please consider that if the wind blows from the wrong direction, you will easily spray yourself!

**For the rare time that an unfriendly dog approaches you:**

- Do not run as that will trigger their predatory (hunting) instinct.

- Do not swing your walking stick wildly around or throw stones. That will only make the dog more aggressive.

- Never, ever stare a dog in the eyes. That is a warning signal among canines that an "immediate attack is approaching".

**Instead:**

- Look around to see if you can see the dog owner and attract his attention. Most of the time the dog is not poised for attack, it only looks like this for the non-dog-savvy pilgrim.

- If you are in the presumed territory of the dog or near livestock the dog is guarding, retreat slowly in a different direction, but don't turn your back on the dog.

- If you carry a walking stick, keep it calmly close to your body, walk slowly and, to combat your own fear, start to sing or hum with a deep voice. Gospel and blues work best.

- Dogs are easily distracted with food. Simply throw something tasty in the direction opposite from where you want to walk. Pay attention so that your movement doesn't seem threatening to the dog. Throw from below, and do not lift your hands or arms over shoulder height. Nevertheless, there is a real danger that the dog is so grateful for the food donation that he becomes friendly and wants to join you on your pilgrimage to Santiago!

Those who are afraid of these furry canines can try to combat their fear whilst still at home. You don't need to consult a psychologist for this. Many dog trainers offer courses that help people get rid of their fear of dogs and help them to understand doggy language. If you know what a dog's body language really means, for example, aggressive or just curious, things become much less frightening.

## A Typical Pilgrim's Day

Many tips in this book become clear as daylight if you know what a typical pilgrim's day looks like! See below:

### ***Pilgrim's Day***

*Long before the sun rises, you can hear the sound of rustling plastic bags. Flashlights shine through the dark. As soon as it is obvious, or at least suspected, that at least half of the pilgrims are awake, (do they have any other choice?), somebody switches on the main light in the dormitory. You wash your face, clean your teeth and, if possible, prepare a cup of coffee or tea, or at least get one out of a vending machine. You finish packing your backpack and off you go, a pilgrim ready to tackle the next stage. In one of the next villages you stop for breakfast, or buy something for a wayside snack. Lunch is either eaten as a picnic on the Way, or in one of the numerous bars and restaurants that you will pass. Quickly, quickly walks the pilgrim to avoid the heat in the middle of the day. Early afternoon, after an average of 15 miles /25 kilometres, you reach the next pilgrim's refugio. You choose a bed, wash pilgrim and clothes, hang your clothes on the lines, check kitchen for provided cooking equipment and go shopping. Explore the village or town, visit the Church or go to mass, go out to a restaurant for dinner or go back to the refuge and cook for yourself or with others. Chat with your fellow pilgrims, perhaps eat together, take your clothes off the washing line, write in your journal/diary, plan tomorrow's stage by re-reading the guide book yet again, pre-pack as much as possible in your backpack and then go to bed. Hopefully you are able to sleep as there is nearly always a world-master snorer sharing the dormitory with you!*

\*\*\*

And the next morning this starts all over again. On the Camino, the pilgrim is focused on the essentials: walk, drink, eat, wash, sleep. And this is exactly what you should keep in mind when you pack your backpack. Concentrate on the essentials - luxury is far too heavy!

# Different Kinds of Pilgrims

No, this is not yet another discussion about "who is a real pilgrim" and who is not - it is an explanation of the different types of pilgrims that exist, of the different ways of doing a pilgrimage, and how all this influences the packing of your backpack.

### *Peregrino* - Standard Pilgrim

The "Standard Pilgrim", also called the traditional pilgrim, is the most frequent pilgrim species found on the Camino. He carries his own backpack and walks alone, or with a few friends, along the main route, the Camino Francés. Some start in France, but what they all have in common is that they walk for a few weeks and carry all their own luggage. As these pilgrims are, statistically, the main group, this books focuses on them and their needs. I have also added, where relevant, points that might be interesting for the following groups.

### Secondary Route Pilgrim

A secondary route pilgrim is one that wants to avoid the crowds on the main route (Camino Francés), especially during the main season, and chooses a less frequented route. For these pilgrims, a good Camino guide, and sometimes even maps and a GPS, are especially important. Secondary routes often have a less developed infrastructure when it comes to *refugios* and places to eat or to buy food. Also ATM machines can be sparse. The right Camino guide warns pilgrims of such "less equipped" stages. Also the weather can be more inclement than on the Camino Francés. The pilgrim, for example, who is determined to walk the *Via de la Plata*, (from

Seville in Southern Spain, up to Galicia in the north), has to be able to carry more water and needs far stronger sun protection. The pilgrim who instead chooses to walk the Camino del Norte, (the Northern Route that follows the Northern shoreline of Spain, along the Bay of Cantabria), in winter, needs to be equipped for colder weather such as snow and ice and has to realize that some *refugios* may be closed.

## Long Distance Pilgrim

This (usually European) pilgrim species is on foot for months, not merely weeks. They start at home and, sometimes, walk back home. I, myself, have met a pilgrim in Spain who started his pilgrimage in the midst of Finland and another one who came by bike from Jerusalem! The equipment for long distance pilgrims is principally the same as for those who are "just" walking a few hundred kilometres. However, as these pilgrims are walking during several seasons and are crossing territories with little pilgrim specific infrastructure, it can be useful to pack more (see chapters on equipment below) and/or to send some of their equipment ahead or back home as the need for it arises or diminishes.

## Luxury Pilgrim

The luxury pilgrim comes in two versions: either with lots of money and/or with an accompanying vehicle. He typically stays in hotels, meaning that he doesn't need to carry a sleeping bag or a towel. If a vehicle is ferrying the heavy luggage forward, this pilgrim only needs to walk with a small day pack containing the essentials such as water, food for the day, and sun protection.

## *Bicigrino* - Pilgrim on a bike

A *bicigrino* can belong to any of the groups above. Besides being on a bike, the main differences is that not only does he have to pack and transport his gear but also all necessary items for bike maintenance and repair.

## Last Minute Pilgrims

Some pilgrims plan for ages, others just head off on a whim. While this book often makes reference to the need for preparation and planning, you can also just buy your gear and head off tomorrow to walk the Camino! If you have the time do some planning, preparation and training - great! If you don't have time for this and plan to start your pilgrimage in the very near future, you will learn on the Way.

## Which Route and When?

Besides your available time and method of transport, (own feet, hooves, wheels), another point to consider is the topography of the specific route and how the weather will most likely be during the time of your pilgrimage. Most pilgrims start in Spain and select the Camino Francés - however there are other routes. Here is a summary of the Camino Francés plus a few thoughts regarding the other pilgrimage routes.

Please bear in mind that the actual start of a pilgrimage is always from the door of your own home; all other starting points are a compromise that most of us have to accept due to available time and money and the location of where we live (hello Australians!).

### Camino Francés

This is the pilgrimage route most think of when they hear "Camino de Santiago". The route starts in France, hence the name, and the Spanish part starts in the Pyrenees.

The three French pilgrimage routes, which start in Le Puy, in Vezelay, and in Paris, unite in Ostabat, France and then continue as the Camino de Navarra from St. Jean-Pied-de-Port over the Pyrenees and into Spain. The route that starts at Arles, in the South-East of France, leads over the Somport Pass and is called the Camino Aragones. Both routes unite in Puente la Reina and are called from here on, the Camino Francés, the pilgrimage route that most people know.

What this means is that some mountain passes have to be climbed. The highest point on the Camino de Navarra is the Ibaneta pass at 1053m (3455 feet) and on the Camino Aragones it is the Puerto de Somport at 1640m (5380 ft). And there are more mountains to climb and plains to hike across further along this route. Therefore you can describe the Camino Francés as a high-plain hiking path with some steeper stages.

Despite all this, you will not need any mountaineering gear, but should be averagely fit and healthy, or at least have your own health problems well under control.

In general it can be said that the Camino Francés is one of the pilgrimage routes that has the best infrastructure for pilgrims (way marking, *refugios,* etc.) and that it is therefore the most recommended for first time pilgrims. Its weather can be described as follows:

Snow and ice can occur in all the mountainous areas until May and can start again as early as September. During the real winter period, it is not advisable to cross the Pyrenees from St. Jean Pied-de-Port via the mountain path but rather to take the valley route. Deaths have occurred! During summer, the weather, especially in the middle part from Burgos to Léon (the Meseta), can be very hot and you have to carry a large water supply. Rain is here less frequent during summer, but in Galicia, rain is abundant during all seasons! Below are the average high and low temperatures for a selected range of places on the Camino Francés. Please bear in mind that these are average temperatures. It can therefore be much hotter or colder whilst you are on the Way.

- January: Roncesvalles (0C/8C - 32F/46F), Léon (-1C/7C - 30F/46F) and Santiago (2C/10C - 35F/50F)
- April: Roncesvalles (5C/16C - 41F/61F), Léon (3C/14C - 37F/57F) and Santiago (4C/15C - 39F/59F)
- July: Roncesvalles (15C/26C - 59F/79F), Léon (12C/27C - 54F/81F) and Santiago (12C/23C - 54F/73F)
- October: Roncesvalles (8C/18C - 46F/64F), Léon (6C/16C - 43F/61F) and Santiago (7C/18C - 45F/64F)

Those that start their pilgrimage in winter, need to be aware that some *refugios* will be closed and that not all of those that are open have central, or any, heating at all. On the other hand, a winter pilgrimage is much quieter and perhaps more authentic, especially since the people who live along the Way have more time and intention to chat with passing pilgrims. (Even if they don't speak anything else other than Spanish and the pilgrim may have no Spanish at all!)

As a **summary** it can be said that the weather is best (most probably) in April, May, June, September and October. July and August are too hot weather-wise and the Camino is far too overcrowded in these two summer months. The pilgrim experience can be the most authentic in winter, from November to February, but is also harder and puts more strain on the pilgrim and his equipment. Also mountainous areas might be covered by snow, making the way markings difficult or impossible to find. If you are not an experienced winter hiker and / or don't speak enough Spanish to ask the locals for advice this can, and has led, to dangerous situations.

### Via de la Plata

The Way from Seville (Southern Spain) to Santiago de Compostela (Galicia) is perhaps the second best one when it comes to pilgrim specific infrastructure. Summers are very hot here (40C+/110F+) the stages between *refugios*, or any type of accommodation, can sometimes be long and water supplies can, especially in summer, be a problem. You will need to consider that very few people that live alongside this route speak anything other than Spanish. If you are not reasonably fluent in the language, you will be in for a lonely and difficult pilgrimage as the other pilgrims on this route will be also mostly Spaniards. Communicating with the locals is important, especially when it comes to reading signs (the route goes through a major breeding area for fighting bulls!). On the positive side, the Way starts in fairly flat territory and slowly builds to a more mountainous terrain. Spring is especially lovely on the *Via de la Plata* with flowers covering the meadows in a breathtaking way while the landscape can be burnt and brown in autumn after the, usually, very hot summer. Absolutely avoid this route in the midst of summer! This route is better suited for pilgrims that speak Spanish to some degree and love solitude.

## Camino del Norte

The northern route is quite mountainous and *refugios* can be sparse. Winter is longer and harsher, summer shorter, and precipitation heavier and much more frequent than on the Camino Francés, especially in Galicia and Asturias. Again, few people here will speak anything other than Spanish (or Basque), and perhaps some French.

## Other Caminos

There are other Caminos in Spain, and France for that matter, as for example those coming up from Madrid or Barcelona or a variant of the Via de la Plata that starts in Granada. These ways have typically even less pilgrim infrastructure and are better suited for those that have already walked the Camino Francés and speak reasonable Spanish.

## Summary - Ideal Time to Travel

On all the routes mentioned above, July and August should be avoided if possible because of the heat and number of pilgrims. The best times for all routes are May/June and September / October. Also keep in mind that winter lasts longer on the Camino del Norte (Northern Route) and that the Via de la Plata (Silver Route) can be unbearably hot even in spring and autumn.

# Spanish Holidays and Vacations

***Pilgrim Anecdote***

*It was my first winter as a hospitalera on the Camino and I really didn't expect huge numbers of pilgrims in the beginning of December. Therefore I went on my way to the parish office to make some photocopies that I needed. Anyone who knows rural Spain knows that a simple walk through the village that shouldn't take more than 10 minutes normally takes "somewhat" longer. You meet the neighbours and if you don't chat with each of them for a little while, they are easily offended. I returned to the refugio two hours later to find it was heaving with pilgrims! What was going on? Día de la Inmaculada Concepcion! It was the Roman-Catholic feast day of the Immaculate Conception, December 8th, a holiday in Spain.*

\*\*\*

Many Spaniards try to walk the Camino in short stages; over weekends, long weekends and vacations. If a holiday falls on a weekday such as a Tuesday or a Thursday, they like to build a *"puente"* (bridge) and make it into a four day long weekend, just enough time to cover another 60 km or so on their ongoing pilgrimage to Santiago.

Here is a list of the relevant Spanish holidays in the **low** season so that you are not surprised when you meet many new pilgrims and find the *refugios* filling up in a time of the year that is otherwise considered to be quiet.

- Christmas, New Year and January 6th (Epiphany / Day of the Three Kings). These are often combined and make up a small extra pilgrim's season in Winter.
- May 1st - Labour Day
- October 12th - National Holiday
- November 1st- All Saints Day
- December 6th - Constitution Day
- December 8th - Immaculate Conception

The actual "pilgrim's season" starts with Holy Week, (the week leading up to Easter Day), and lasts until mid/end of October, so during this "high season" additional holidays make less of an impact as there is continual high pilgrim traffic on the Camino.

If you start before or in Pamplona you should avoid the city between the 6th and 14th July. These are the days of the *Sanfermines* that Ernest Hemingway immortalized in his novel "Fiesta". Not only are the streets full of celebrating people, and sometimes running bulls, but the hotels are booked up (and charge hyper-prices) and most of the pilgrim's *refugios* in Pamplona and surrounding areas will be closed.

## Day of Travelling and Start of the Pilgrimage

Most pilgrims start on a weekend and that causes a "pilgrim wave" to happen, especially in summer. If you want to avoid this, do the opposite and try to reach the following places (typical starting points) on a weekday in the middle of the week: Saint Jean Pied-de-Port, Roncesvalles, Pamplona, Logroño, Burgos, Léon, Astorga, Ponferrada, O Cebreiro and Sarría.

The pilgrim who follows this advice and thus walks outside the main stream of pilgrims can experience a quieter Camino than somebody that walks with the masses, even at the same time of the year. You should also be aware of the typical stages promoted by many Camino guides that lead many pilgrims automatically to the same *refugios*/towns each night. Once again it is true that those who walk outside of the stream often have it easier!

**These are the typical stages of the Camino Francés which you should try to avoid if possible by stopping between them:**

Roncesvalles > Larrasoaña > Pamplona > Puente la Reina > Estella > Los Arcos > Logroño > Najéra > Santo Domingo de la Calzada > Belorado > San Juan de Ortega > Burgos > Hontanas > Castrojeriz > Fromista > Carrion de los Condes > Terradillos de los Templarios > Sahagun > Reliegos > Léon > Hospital de Orbigo > Astorga > Rabanal del Camino > Ponferrada > Villafranca del Bierzo > O Cebreiro > Triacastela > Sarría > Portomarin > Palas del Rei > Arzua > Monte de Gozo > Santiago de Compostela.

Between all these above villages and towns, are numerous other ones that welcome pilgrims and that are, in general, far less overrun!

## Start of the Camino and available time

How much vacation time you have, where you start, and where and when you hope to arrive, are all things that influence your planning. As a rule of thumb, you should calculate to walk an average of 20 kilometres/12 miles per walking day. This gives you enough margin for rest days. And this means that somebody that has, for example, 22 full walking days available and wants to arrive in Santiago should start 440 kilometres/270 miles before Santiago; in Burgos. If you only have 10 full days available for walking you should start in Ponferrada, etc. And if you are ahead of your schedule, you can always take a rest day, stay a bit longer in Santiago de Compostela or walk on to Finisterre.

What you should avoid at all costs is time pressure. It is the death of the pilgrimage experience. Also keep in mind that you might need additional rest days due to blisters or tendon/joint problems that make walking the next day impossible. Consider the 20km/12mi/day rule of thumb which leaves enough leeway for rest days, although the average daily "coverage" of a pilgrim is closer to 25k/15 mi. There are also pilgrims who discover that their daily distance is less that 20km/12mi/day. Hopefully you have done some training/local walks beforehand and have a sense as to whether or not 15 or 20 km is too much for you.

**One word of caution:** Many pilgrims catch the "Camino bug" and once they have arrived in Santiago after a shorter pilgrimage, they return to walk the other, previously missed stages. It perhaps makes more sense, if possible, to start earlier on the Way and to walk/work your way towards Santiago in several different vacations instead of first experiencing the highlight of the Camino- the arrival in Santiago - and then doing the actual work, the long pilgrimage by foot. This is obviously easier said than done if you are from overseas, but still a valid approach for European pilgrims.

*A good inspiration may be found in the following story of an Austrian Protestant minister I met in Galicia. He had started his Camino from home and walked stages of it during his vacations until he reached - after twelve years - Santiago de Compostela. When I met him in Spain he was already on his way back home, also on foot, and he told me happily that the way back will be so much faster for him as he was now retired!*

\*\*\*

Yes, the Way is the destination, but the destination of the Way is to reach Santiago de Compostela. Those who arrive first at the destination and then later walk the Way miss out on many things. At least in my opinion.

## Technology and a Thousand Years Old Pilgrimage Route

A modern cell phone can be very useful and can almost replace a laptop and a digital camera. But does it, and other electronic gadgets, belong on the Camino, or do they distract more than they are useful? Do you really need them? Both points of view have their pros and cons. The only one who can make this decision is the pilgrim in question - you. Here are my thoughts on the subject:

Modern cell phones (smart phones) are like tools - they can be useful as well as not. The Camino offers the pilgrim a unique opportunity to let go, to concentrate on those things that are really important, to contemplate our modern world from the outside, and to evaluate ones own attitude towards many modern amenities. Those that are addicted to the internet, update their Facebook status hourly, tweet each of their movements and are, in general, more at home in cyberspace than in the real world, should toy with the idea of walking the Camino as an internet detox-route.

On the other hand, a cell phone can replace many other pieces of equipment; for example a camera. eBooks can be uploaded to it, maps, translation apps, language guides and dictionaries and even the Bible can be taken with you without adding more weight. And obviously, it also serves as a phone for emergencies, or to tell friends and family at home that you still have not been eaten by the wild Spanish dogs.

If you are walking the Camino during the low season or have chosen one of the less frequented routes, you should take a simple cell phone to a) call the person that opens/has the key to the *refugio* (*hospitaleros* are not always sitting in the *refugios* waiting for a pilgrim to arrive, especially if there is "little traffic" on the road) and b) for emergency calls in case you sprain your ankle and can't hobble on.

If you need to stay in contact with your dearest at home, for example, or if there is a real chance of an emergency at home that would necessitate you ending the pilgrimage and travelling home, then you should take a phone with very basic functions; mainly receiving and sending texts and calls. If you want to go "full detox", leave all electronic gadgets at home. If you feel it will not distract you from the Camino experience and you want to save weight on books etc, take a modern smart phone that replaces several other pieces of equipment.


**Staying in Contact**

What is cheaper and better? To buy a local, prepaid SIM card or phone in Spain, or to use the roaming provided by your telephone contract from home? This is a topic experts and pilgrims discuss without end. It all depends on where you are from and what your telephone needs are.

One thing you need to do before leaving home is to ask your telephone provider how much calls and texts from Spain to home and vice versa will cost. Don't forget that calls from your home country abroad to your phone will be charged as international roaming calls. Deciding whether to use your phone just as you do at home or buy a Spanish SIM card or phone, depends on how often you plan to use it and for what.

If you only send the very occasional "Hi, I am still alive" SMS to your nearest and dearest at home, then you might not save much money by getting a local SIM card or phone. If you call home often and talk at length, but don't receive many calls from home, you will find a local SIM card or phone to be cheaper. SIM cards, or even whole simple phones, can be found in Spain on nearly every corner, or at least in one of the many electronic shops, and in the railway stations/airports of the most frequent points of entry into Spain. Don't forget, if you decide to take your cell phone, and any other electronic gadget, you will also need the respective chargers and plug adapters. These also add to your total weight. Consider the purchase of a single, universal charger for all the electronic things that you plan to take. You will also need an adapter from USA/Canada, or the UK/Ireland, or New Zealand/Australia, to plug in all of your chargers in Spain.

Another way of saving costs on calls are VOIP services like Skype. Check if your phone is smart enough to work with Skype or similar! And if you have decided to take an iPad or netbook with you on the Camino, you should install Skype on it and tell your family and friends at home to do the same. If you only want to check your email very occasionally it is best to do this in the quite common internet cafés rather than carrying heavy technology in your backpack. Also Wi-Fi hotspots are now common in *refugios* and bars/restaurants along the way; just bear in mind basic internet security and be aware of which information you send from your device via an unsecured network!

What should, in my opinion, be left at home are iPods and similar music machines. They distract from the sounds and silence of the Camino and they can cut you off from fellow pilgrims and the people that live along the Way. To (re-)discover silence is one of the biggest gifts/treasures you can find on the Camino. Consider giving yourself this gift.

## Every Gram Counts

Already our grandmothers knew that "A lot of little makes a lot." In a pilgrim's backpack, grams and ounces quickly add up to kilos and pounds. Nevertheless I have avoided giving concrete figures for each piece of equipment as it is of little use for you to know how much my own sleeping bag weighs. It is much more important for you to know what a good average weight for a sleeping bag would be, as this helps you to make an informed buying decision.

To weigh your gear, piece by piece, you can either use kitchen or office scales. To weigh the whole, fully packed backpack, or bigger pieces of equipment, you can use your bathroom scales. In the appendix of this book you will find a link to a page on my website where you can download customizable packing lists both as pdf and doc files which can be adjusted by you, depending on your personal needs. They have an extra column where you can note the weight of each piece of your equipment. This way you can keep an overview of what weighs how much and where there might be some leeway to save a few more ounces.

Only one pound more or less can make a big difference in your pilgrim experience. Please bear in mind that you will carry your whole backpack every day and over an average distance of 25 km / 15 mi on each of these days. That is around 30,000 steps each day that you spend carrying your backpack. I promise that you will be glad about each ounce left behind and angry with yourself about each gram too many!

One of the riches of the pilgrimage lies in the reflection about what is and isn't necessary, and in the learning to distinguish between important and unimportant things.

The more often you walk the Camino, the clearer it becomes that those things that we cannot see, and that weigh nothing, are often more important than the tangible possessions we carry in our backpacks.

## There are shops in Spain - Really!

Sometimes it is unbelievable what pilgrims bring from home to the Camino: Food for the first few days isn't the worst! Really, there are shops in Spain in which you can buy everything you need, not always the same brand as at home, but a similar product. No need, for example, for female pilgrims to bring a whole months supply of sanitary pads or tampons. They are available in every shop in Spain!

When you run out of something, simply ask for the *supermercado* (supermarket), or, in villages, for the *tienda* (grocery / corner shop). In the following bigger towns, which are all on the Camino Francés, you will find everything, and more, that you would find in a town in your home country: Pamplona, Logroño, Burgos, Léon, Ponferrada and Santiago de Compostela. But even in smaller villages and towns, everything that a pilgrim wants and really needs is readily available.

The pilgrimage to Santiago has a more than 1,000 year long history. The shopkeepers along the way are therefore used to catering for the pilgrim's needs!

## General thoughts about the necessary equipment

### Do you really have to buy completely new equipment?

No, absolutely not! If you already own walking boots that are used to your feet and vice versa, a backpack that is comfortable to carry, and a good pocket knife, then take them with you. Nevertheless, it might be a good idea to check the respective chapters in this book to see if the equipment you have is adequate for the Camino. Heavy mountaineering boots are, for example, only necessary in the midst of winter. In all other seasons sturdy walking boots are more than enough.

### Where should you buy your equipment?

Items that have to be tried on personally, like boots and backpack, should be bought in a good, specialized outdoor shop and not on-line. Other things can be bought on-line without a problem and can sometimes save you a chunk of money. In the appendix there are some useful addresses of on-line shops that have worked for me for many years.

**Extra Tips**: If you find a pair of boots that fit perfectly or a good fitting backpack in an outdoor shop it might be a good idea to check its on-line prices from other retailers and the manufacturer itself. Especially if you are are on a tight budget.

Look out for end of season/discontinued lines sales. You don't need to follow the latest fashion if that means you can save some money.

### Second hand or borrowing?

Why not? If you are on a tight budget you should consider buying certain things second hand or borrowing them from friends, family, or acquaintances. But again, bear in mind that the backpack and boots have to really fit you well or your pilgrimage will quickly become "*El Camino de la tortura*", the Way of torture. Things like walking sticks or digital cameras can, if still in good shape, be bought second hand or borrowed without a problem.

**Extra Tip**: If you are a member of a pilgrim's association it might pay to check with them to see if they run some sort of "gear exchange" event. If they don't, you can always suggest that they do!

## What do you need to buy first and what should you buy last?

The thing you need to apply for first is your pilgrim's passport (*credencial*) and what you need to buy first are your walking boots and your Camino guide. It can take several weeks and up to months for your *credencial* application to be processed by the respective association and you need to break in your boots thoroughly before starting your pilgrimage. The guide should be purchased well ahead so that you can read up on what to expect and what type of gear you might or might not need on that particular Camino.

The next thing on your shopping list should be your sleeping bag, as this typically takes up the most space in your backpack. Buy the backpack last, but at least a few weeks before actually starting, as it depends on the rest of your equipment as to how big your backpack needs to be. And everything else? In between! In the ideal case you should have your whole gear together several weeks before you start your pilgrimage. This way you can train with your actual equipment on your shoulders, discover any weak points and mistakes early on, and correct them.

## Gender Separation?

One thing that worries a lot of pilgrims is the question: Are there separated dormitories, bathrooms and toilets in the *refugios* or not? As the Galicians would say "*¡Depende!*" - It depends!

### ***Pilgrim Anecdote***

*It was on my very first Camino and I was spending the evening in my very first refugio when I discovered that the hospitalero had obviously decided that there were too few pilgrims during the low season to keep two bathrooms clean and open, so we had unisex toilets and showers. Granted, first it is strange, but after a few refugios I discovered that nobody actually cared about my body.*

*They were all far more concerned about taking care of their own blisters and aching feet!*

\*\*\*

- Most of the *refugios* do have gender separated toilets and bathrooms/showers, especially during the main season.
- And if not, the majority of showers have some sort of curtain or door before the shower stall, so that you can get undressed "out of view".
- Another option, if the need arises, is to team up with your fellow pilgrims and agree who goes first in the shower, the boys or the girls, while the others are "guarding" the door, and vice versa.
- It is completely normal to see pilgrims of both sexes in the same dormitory and yes, especially in summer, sparsely dressed/getting undressed for the night. It will only take you a few days to get used to it.
- No matter what your creed is, we were all born naked and without clothes on. Remember that and relax. If you go to the beach people are typically wearing less than the pilgrims in a *refugio* dormitory.
- The less you look at other pilgrims in these situations, the less they will look at you.

## Women specific pilgrim tips

If you don't normally wear a bra, consider buying one or two good sport bras with wide shoulder straps as you will appreciate the given support.

Women with long hair or a high maintenance hair style should consider changing their hairstyle to something more "easy care". Long hair needs a lot of water for washing and more time to dry - important points especially in winter!

I know it is unjust, but men's sportswear is often cheaper than women's. Nobody will notice if you wear "male" walking trousers.

If you don't normally take the pill, you might want to discuss this with your doctor to see if it would make sense to take it during the Camino. With hormonal contraception, the menstruation is often lighter, less painful, and can even be "scheduled" to a certain degree. If you have only two weeks to enjoy the Camino, it can make a big difference if you can experience these days without your "days".

Tampons are much more practical and hygienic on the Camino, especially in summer, than any other method of female hygiene I know of.

Waxing your legs is a fashion, and even the most fashion conscious *peregrina* should consider if it is really worth the extra weight to take the required things with her. If you decide to let your hair grow as nature does, start at home at least one week prior to starting your Camino. When the hair under the arms grows back, it prickles and if combined with sweat and heat - you will soon notice what I am referring to …

Many women are afraid to walk the Camino alone. I have walked over 6,000 km /3700 mi on European pilgrim ways, most of the time as a solo woman. All this considered, I cannot remember one single incident where I did not feel safe. Many other female pilgrims have confirmed this experience over the years in conversations with me. This means I am not a single case, but only one of many. Woman are rarely really alone on the Camino, unless you are walking in the midst of winter, as there are lots of other pilgrims around! The main danger on the Camino is more likely a sprained ankle or blisters than "bad men".

## Men specific pilgrim tips

Men should consider leaving their shaving gear at home and just grow a beard. This saves weight in your backpack and keeps your face warmer, especially when temperatures are lower. It is recommended to start growing the beard at home before you leave.

If you have problems finding a backpack that fits because you have a shorter back than the average male, try one that was made specifically for women. Nobody will know that you found your ideal backpack in the ladies department of the outdoor store - as long as you don't choose a pink one!

Wallets don't belong in your back pocket! The danger of loss and theft on the Way and in the *refugios* is comparatively low, but to carry your wallet, or anything else of value, in your back pocket is still not a good idea.


## LGBTQ Tips

You might have difficulty believing it, but Spain is actually a pretty tolerant country, despite the fact that Roman-Catholicism is nearly the "state religion". A Spanish saying to illustrate the latter point: *"In Spain we are all Roman-Catholics, even the atheists."* Legal, same-sex civil partnerships have existed in Spain since 2005 and the adoption of children by LGBTQ couples is possible. Further, in a 2007 survey, 82% of the population answered, "Yes!" to the question asking if society should accept homosexuality.

Nevertheless, there are a few things LGBTQ pilgrims should consider. Even in a heterosexual context is it not considered "good form" in Spain to show affection too obviously in public. This means walking hand in hand on the Camino is OK, but to eat each other with kisses will cause raised eyebrows, independent of the gender combination. Accommodation on the Camino is typically in dormitories in *refugios,* so if you would like something more private, head to a hotel room.

And no, there is not much of a gay or lesbian subculture on the Camino. Only a pilgrim culture which, in general, tries to be as inclusive as possible, independent of skin colour or sexual orientation. So, discrimination doesn't exist on the Camino at all? Yes, sadly it does, but rarely. Those who wait until every other human being on the planet accepts him as he is will have to wait a long time.

**Summary**: LGBTQ people, and other minorities, have as little problems (or the same problems, depending on how you look at it) on the Camino as in their home countries. Nevertheless, stating the fact straight into the face of the local Roman-Catholic parish priest might not be a good idea; though sometimes you might be surprised. Here is it advisable to let common sense, the least common of all senses, reign.

## General Tips for Weight Reduction

### Combinations and Multi-Use Purposes of Your Gear

Apart from weighing your gear and buying the lightest model available or affordable, this is perhaps the most important tip to achieve a light weight pilgrim's backpack. Here are a few examples:

- A modern cell phone/smart phone can replace your address book, camera, Camino guide (use the free Kindle app), flashlight, watch, alarm clock, date/calendar book or diary and much more.

- A pareo/sarong (see below) can be used as a towel, skirt, swimming costume, picnic blanket, scarf, sun protection, etc.

- The same shower gel can be used to wash your body, hair, and clothes. No reason to carry extra shampoo or soap.

- Sun cream can also serve as normal skin cream.

Ask yourself every single time if something you want to take with you can fulfil multiple purposes or if it only does one thing. Try to cover as many uses as possible with as few items as possible.

### Clever packing is lighter packing

With the following tips, if applied rigorously, you can easily reduce the final weight of your backpack by up to 1 kg. Collect all that you cut off or rip off at the end and weigh it. You will be surprised by how much weight you will have saved with the following tips!

If you decide to us a printed version of the Camino guide rather than an electronic one, cut out all the pages that you will not need on the way, like those about preparation or those about the stages you have already walked. **Extra Tip**: Cut the pages out leaving a few millimetres still attached to the binding. If you just rip them out completely, the integrity of the book binding might be compromised and the book may fall apart.

Remove redundant labels, clips, straps, etc. from your backpack and clothes - just make sure before you do this that they really don't fulfil an use that you might need.

Save necessary addresses and telephone numbers in your cell phone or on a single sheet of paper and leave the heavy address book at home. This also allows you to carry your important addresses/emails in a single page in your money belt.

Again, examine every piece of your gear and see if there is something dangling from it that you don't need and can remove without danger to its function.

Always choose the smallest, simplest, and lightest version of something. For example, use a mini toothbrush instead a regular sized one, buy toothpaste in travel size, and take a comb or a mini brush instead of your big hairbrush that you use at home.

Don't take any large supplies of anything. If you use up your mini toothpaste, you can easily buy a new one in Spain. Remember - there are shops in Spain - really!

If you travel to the Camino by plane, please keep in mind the rules and regulations regarding what can and can't go into your carry-on luggage. Refer to your airline's website for detailed advice as these rules change frequently. As a rule of thumb, anything sharp and anything that could be used as a weapon, has to be in checked-in luggage, even your nail scissors. Also, the amount of liquids that you are allowed to carry on in your hand luggage is restricted to 100ml/3oz each in bottles of a maximum size of 3.4 oz and has to go in a clear plastic bag of not more than 1 quart (.95L) or 7 x 8 in or 17.8 x 20.3 cm !

**Summary**

With every piece of gear you want to pack, ask yourself the following questions:

- What is the worst that can happen if I do NOT take this with me? The answer determines if you need to pack it or if you can leave it at home.

- Can I remove anything from this to decrease its weight without decreasing its function?

- Can I replace several pieces of equipment with one that combines several functions in one?

**Reducing weight on the Way**

No, I am not speaking about the weight reduction that happens around your waistline. I am talking about how to make sure that the weight in your backpack or your bike panniers, does not increase slowly over time because of small things "sneaking in".

*\*\*\*Pilgrim Anecdote\*\*\**

*During my first pilgrimage I walked from time to time with a Swiss pilgrim. Even then it was my habit to empty my backpack completely every two to three days, to throw everything away that I didn't need anymore and to re-pack it carefully. My dear co-pilgrim found this always very amusing and, for him, a waste of time because he didn't have anything superfluous in his pack - at least so he thought. We happened to reach Santiago together and as he had booked a flight home, he decided, because of the danger of extra charges for extra weight, to finally check his backpack. A full three kilos of "nothing superfluous in my backpack" saw the light of day! It is amazing how fast things accumulate in a backpack or bike pannier; the pamphlet describing the Church you visited, the entrance ticket to an exhibition, the restaurant bills ... All these little pieces add up over the weeks!*

\*\*\*

**Therefore here is the next important tip:**

Empty your pack every two or three days, examine it for damage, especially the seams, zips and belts, and re-pack it completely. Every little souvenir you find and know that you do not need anymore should be thrown away, or, if you want to keep it for nostalgic reasons, mail it home (expensive) or by *poste restante* to Santiago (cheaper, but see respective section below).

## Pilgrims with Animals

The pilgrim who walks the Camino with an animal companion sometimes has it easier, but more often finds it more difficult. Donkeys and horses are used by a few hundred pilgrims each year as a transport vehicle. Even more try to take their dog on the Camino. It is important to know that dogs, aside from certified seeing-eye or assistance dogs, are **NOT** allowed in the *refugios* on the way. And apart from that, you will need to carry not only your own equipment, but also that of your canine companion.

Pilgrims who plan to walk the Camino with an animal companion should think thrice about it! Food and accommodation are difficult to find and the travel back home can be difficult to arrange! Here is what did work for three Spanish pilgrims - grandfather, father, and son:

*\*\*\*Pilgrim Anecdote\*\*\**

*These three had started from home, had a donkey with them to carry part of their luggage and a dog that guarded everything. Guarding is saying too much as that dog was so friendly that the only danger was being licked to death by him. These pilgrims tried to avoid the bigger towns, or at least to cross them as quickly as possible early or late in the day when there was less traffic, and tried to find a welcome in smaller places where they would typically pitch their tents on a meadow close to the refugio. This way they could use the facilities of the refugios, the shower, toilet, and kitchen, and had few problems with accommodating their four-legged companions on the village meadow. The donkey carried, amongst other things, the two tents; a big one for the humans and a small one for the dog.*

\*\*\*

***

*Heinrich, a seasoned hippie, who started walking in Austria, had a donkey with him that carried the equipment, including a flower vase and knitting gear. When I met them in the middle of Spain, they were so used to each other that most of the time the donkey walked by Heinrich's side without a lead - like an over-sized dog.*

***

In both cases the pilgrims had several things in common. They were fluent in Spanish which facilitated the communication with the person that owned the field/meadow or with the neighbours/people that live alongside the way. They also had enough time and thus no time pressures and could therefore walk calmly and without over exercising their companion animals. And in both cases, they not only had started from home, but also planned to walk back home!

Donkeys are, obviously, easier to feed than horses. Those who plan to do the Camino with a horse will either need an accompanying vehicle to transport food, mobile paddock and the like, or will need to plan well ahead and know where feed for a horse can be bought. You also will need to know where you can find a blacksmith. And how will your horse or donkey make the journey back home? All of these logistics have to be figured out before the first hoof touches the Camino!

Both donkeys and horses can manage the Camino with enough time and good planning provided, but with dogs things get even more complicated! As already mentioned, dogs, with the exception of certified seeing eye and assistance dogs are **NOT** allowed in the pilgrim *refugios* and walking through Spanish villages with them can prove to be a challenge. The resident village dogs are generally not amused if a strange dog tries to cross their territory. Add to this that the average daily stage of 20 km/12 mi that a pilgrim walks daily translates easily into 30km/17 for a dog that is not leashed and thus is walking and running back and forth. This will repeat every day on your Camino. After considering all this, you will likely realize that it is, nearly always better to leave your dog at home.

If you still insist on taking your dog on pilgrimage, you should choose a "quiet" season and should not plan to walk more than 15 km/9 mi per day. You will also need to carry a tent as even most hotels and *pensions* in Spain will not allow a dog in the room. Plus, the dog needs to be trained and to belong to a breed that a) likes to walk and b) is big enough to do this kind of exercise and c) can cope well with heat and cold.

As well, the travel back home from Santiago is difficult, as dogs are not allowed on the buses and trains; again the only exception being certified seeing-eye and assistance dogs or, in some cases, very small dogs in a transport box. Therefore you need to figure out, before you even start to walk with your dog, how you will get your dog home in the end.

## Food, Drink and Water

The Spaniards have a saying *"Con pan y vino se anda el camino"* which can be translated as "With bread and wine you walk the Camino" (nearly effortlessly).

### Mealtimes

The daily pilgrims' routine and that of the people that live alongside the Camino differ like night and day from each other when it comes to meal times.

This is especially noticeable in that many restaurants don't start serving evening meals until 9 pm and whose kitchen is therefore closed at the earlier time when you would like to eat dinner.

Over the years this has changed for the better on the more popular Camino routes and many bars and restaurants have adapted their opening hours to pilgrims' needs.

- You will be hard pressed to find breakfast served before 09:00 unless you stay in a hotel or (private) *refugio* that serves it.
- Lunch is typically served between 13:00 to 15:00 (or even later).
- Dinner often doesn't start until 21:00 at the earliest.

## Breakfast

You normally need to leave the *refugio* by 08:00. Solution: If the *refugio* doesn't offer breakfast, you need to buy some food for breakfast the previous day to eat before you head off and look for a second breakfast, with a nice, hot *café con leche* (latte / coffee with hot milk) in one of the villages you will walk through later.

**Extra Tips**: Some *refugios* do offer breakfast and you should take them up on it. But you should, at all costs, avoid the coffee or similar that is sold out of automatic vending machines! To put it politely, they are rarely, in my experience, thoroughly and frequently cleaned. If you ever happen to see one of these open, you'll know what I mean.

Many bars serve *Tortilla Española* which is a potato and egg "omelet". Though it is traditionally served as a *tapa* item, it is often available early in the day and thus you can have it for breakfast as a good protein and salt hit when you stop in at a bar.

## Lunch or Dinner

## Picnic Lunch/Snacks

Cured sausage (*chorizo*), cheese, bread, dried fruit, nuts, chocolate, yoghurt, bananas, etc. can be bought in nearly every village and make for a great wayside picnic in good weather. Bananas are especially important as they contain minerals like potassium that prevent muscle cramps. Sausage and cheese take care of your necessary salt intake. Remember, you not only lose water when sweating, but also salt and other minerals.

Bananas and nuts are two of the best foods I know of to prevent muscle cramps and low blood sugar and you should eat them daily. I also suggest carrying a few mixed nuts and dried fruit in your back pack (*frutos secos* in Spanish) in case of low blood sugar in between villages/bars.

## Daily Menu or Pilgrim's Menu

These are two names for the same thing. They cost around 10 Euros and are available in many bars, restaurants and private *refugios*, both for lunch and dinner. They typically consist of three courses (salad/soup/pasta, then a meat or fish dish, sometimes with fries, and finally dessert) and include bread and wine, water or soft-drinks. You may want to eat your main meal of the day for lunch (which is typical in Spain) depending on how much longer you plan to walk after having eaten so much. Alternatively, in many bars along the way you can buy a *bocadillo* (a baguette style sandwich) if you don't feel like eating a huge lunch nor like having a self-catered picnic along the Way. You can buy a *bocadillo* any time of day.

**Alcohol-free Beer** (*cerveza sin alcohol* in Spanish) is perhaps the best drink for pilgrims to order with your menu or *bocadillo* at lunchtime. It is full of healthy minerals, and, being alcohol free, allows you to walk on without being tipsy. Wine is better left for the evenings.


## Shopping and Cooking

Many *refugios* have a kitchen which is available for the pilgrims. Before you start off on your shopping trip, you need to first check what kind of cooking gear and food basics (i.e. olive oil, salt) are provided in the *refugio*. Another good idea is to team up with other pilgrims and shop, cook, and eat together. This not only saves money, but is also easier and more fun than every single pilgrim trying to cook his own meal in an often small and cramped kitchen.

**Note:** Businesses in Spain, including smaller grocery stores, are open Monday to Friday from approximately 9:30 - 13:00 and then again from 16:30 - 20:30. Larger grocery stores stay open from 9:30 through to 20:30. On Saturday many businesses close at 13:00 and do not re-open for the afternoon. On Sunday, almost everything is closed except for perhaps a bakery or a small "corner" store, but these are again only open in the morning.


## Salt

A balanced salt/water intake is important to prevent many heat related problems like cramps. Many pilgrims not only make the mistake of not drinking enough water, but also often forget to eat enough salt to replace that lost by sweating. Without salt, the water you drink doesn't "stay" in the body but rather gets excreted almost immediately and a vicious circle develops that can lead to muscle cramps, dizziness, or even fainting.

Worse than that can be the so-called water intoxication (hypotone/hyper-hydration). This happens when a lot of water is drunk but no salt or other minerals are taken in. The symptoms start with dizziness, being confused, nausea and vomiting (which increases the problem!) and can go as far as damage to internal organs (especially the kidneys) and in extreme cases even death through brain oedema.

I myself always carry a very small container of salt in my belt pouch so that I have it readily accessible. If I notice any dizziness I take a pinch of salt, and as long as the salt tastes good, I know I need a little bit more. As soon as it starts to taste bad, I know my body has enough for the moment. This, together with sufficient water intake (see below), has always worked well for me. Obviously, eating salt and mineral rich food as a picnic or trail snack, also helps.

## Vegetarians and Vegans

### ***Pilgrim Anecdote***

*They were a lovely couple from New Zealand and they both spoke word perfect Spanish. Both were also strict vegetarians, but after cooking for weeks for themselves in the refugio kitchens, they thought it would be a nice change to have a restaurant meal. They took great care to explain to the waiter the situation and repeated frequently that they wouldn't eat any meat at all. In the end they settled for a nice plate of different vegetables and salads. The salads were fine, but the vegetables were lavishly covered with fried bacon. They called the waiter back and complained saying that they had ordered food without meat in it, to which the waiter replied: "¡Pero eso no es carne - es pancetta! But that is not meat - that is bacon!"*

\*\*\*

Other Traps for Vegetarians and Vegans include:

* Mixed salad (*ensalada mixta*) is often decorated with hard boiled eggs and canned tuna.

- *Ensaladilla rusa* is a mayonnaise based cooked vegetable salad - often with a hard boiled egg on top.
- *Caldo* (broth) is always meat based while *sopa* (soup) is most of the time, but not always, based on vegetables and is meat free.

To avoid mishaps in restaurants, here is a template to get you started: delete what doesn't apply to you, write it on a piece of paper, and show it to the server. Pray to St. James that it will work and that the server will point to something on the menu that will be safe for you to eat!

*"Soy vegetariano/vegetariana // vegano/vegana y no como productos de origen animal. Ni carne, ni pancetta, ni pescado, ni lácteos, ni huevos, ni miel. ¿Me puede recomendar algo?"*

"I am vegetarian/ / vegan and don't eat any animal products. No meat, no bacon, no fish, no dairy products, no eggs, no honey. Can you recommend something?

**NOTE**: *vegetariano/vegano* are masculine, *vegetariana/vegana* are feminine.

**Extra Tips**:

Fortunately Spain is full of delicious fresh vegetables, fruit, beans, and nuts, though soy products are normally only found in the bigger towns and cities. Protein sources like chickpeas and beans, important for those on a vegan diet, are often sold in tins, cans, or jars and already pre-cooked.

Kitchens in the *refugios* are often small and have little equipment, thus it is best to team up with other pilgrims even if they are not vegetarians or vegans to cook together. Just offer to cook the "healthy" parts of the meal whilst they are taking care of the "carnivorous" parts - problem solved!

***Pilgrim Anecdote***

*A pilgrim arrived at the refugio where I served as a hospitalera and she was a vegetarian. Out of curiosity I asked her how she was finding being a vegetarian on the Camino. She responded that she did fine as she lived on the amazing bread and chocolate in Spain! You see, with a bit of cheerfulness, there is always a way ;-)*

\*\*\*

## Drinking Water

There is no need to buy bottled water in shops in Spain as nearly every village on the Camino has at least one drinking water fountain. If the sign at the fountain says *"potable"*, it means you can drink it. If instead it reads *"NO potable"*, it means it is not safe to drink.

If in doubt, you can always ask the locals; in an emergency, with improvised sign language and pantomime. Tap water is perfectly safe to drink in mainland Spain. Though it contains more chlorine than in many other countries, you will quickly adapt to the new taste. If there is no fountain with drinking water available, it is perfectly OK to show up with your empty water bottle and a friendly *Agua, por favor.* (Water, please.) in the next bar. They will fill it promptly for you with tap water. If there is no bar in sight the neighbours are normally happy to help you, especially if you say *por favor* (please) and *muchas gracias* (many thanks)!

## How much water does a pilgrim need?

More than most pilgrims think! The loss of water suffered by the body through exercise and the higher than you are used to temperature of the environment, means that you need considerably more water than you drink at home. A good indicator if you are drinking enough or not is the colour of your urine. The darker it is, the more you need to drink. But remember, for the body to be able to keep this water and use it, you also need to replace the salt you lose through sweating (see above).

In practical terms, this means the following:

- Before you start in the morning, drink your fill of water and eat something for breakfast that contains salt.
- Depending on the season, weather, and the distance to the next watering hole, you should have at least 0.5 to 1 litre of water in your bottle. You will need even more in summer and/or if the next water hole is far away - (a good Camino guide book will warn you of this).
- Refill your water bottle and yourself at every fountain.
- Don't forget to eat salty things and bananas during the day.

After a few days, you will develop a good body awareness that helps you to judge how much water you will need to carry in your bottle for how many kilometres / miles of walking.

Water is also important for good functioning of your tendons, joints, and ligaments. An orthopaedist on pilgrimage whom I met, told me: "This pain is not an inflammation of the tendons, joints, or ligaments - they are simply thirsty!"

If the body does not have enough water available, it first tries to find the water it needs from somewhere in the body where it is not essential for survival, for example in the production of the synovial fluid (synovium) that surrounds the joints and certain parts of the muscles. The synovial fluid normally consists of up to 94% water and thickens quickly from lack of water in the body. This thickening makes the lubrication of joints and tendons less effective and movements can become painful - aka tendinitis. Thus the best first aid when you feel any such pain is to offer your body more water. Cheers!

## Lack of Water in Spain

Many parts of Spain suffer, especially in summer, from an extreme lack of water. Please keep this in mind when you take a shower or wash your clothes! Every drop of water wasted means that others have less water. In the height of summer in a dry year it can happen, especially in La Rioja and in the Meseta (high plains between Burgos and Leon), that the *hospitalero* greets pilgrims with a 2 litre bottle of water - for your shower. That means that the water table has sunk so low that water has to be brought in by truck from other places! Therefore please don't complain; instead be thankful that the neighbours are still willing to share their very limited water supply with the pilgrim masses.

## Shower and Washing Clothes

If there are a lot of pilgrims in the *refugio* it is possible that there will not be enough hot water for all. Sometimes it is best to just wash quickly and wait for the evening in the hope that the boiler has caught up again and you can take your hot shower then.

**Important:** Spaniards typically shower by turning the water OFF when they are soaping up and lathering. They then turn the water back on to rinse off, rather than leaving the shower running the whole time as we tend to do in North America and in other water-rich areas of the world. This is a good practice to help save both water in general and specifically hot water for pilgrims who shower after you.

When it comes to washing your clothes, remember that your hiking clothes will get just as clean with cold water and the hot water should be preserved for showers for the pilgrims that arrive later on. That is the reason why in most *refugios* there are only cold water taps at the clothes washing basins.

**Extra Tips:** Take your dirty clothes with you in the shower and pre-soak them at your feet whilst washing yourself. After that you can transport them, in a waterproof bag, to the official clothes washing place for final washing and rinsing.

And in case you run out of soap, washing up liquid can be found in most kitchens; a tiny drop of this goes a long way to get your clothes clean.

Some *refugios* have coin or token operated washing machines and dryers available. If you share them with other pilgrims you can save money and the environment.

Most homes in Spain do not have a clothes dryer, but rather dry their clothes outside on the line. You will often only have the clothes line option at the *refugios* for drying your clothes.

# How much should your backpack weigh?

As a rule of thumb, the backpack of a pilgrim should, all included, weigh a maximum 10% (summer) and 15% (winter) of the pilgrim's body weight. (Remember that the backpack itself weighs something, plus the weight of water and food.)

While that is roughly correct, there are exceptions to the rule.

An overweight man who weighs 200 kg should not additionally burden himself with a 20 kg backpack and a petite woman that weighs only 45 kg will have problems packing everything she needs and still staying under 4.5 kg.

Out of experience, I would say that 8 kg in summer and around 10 kg in winter will be more than sufficient to contain all that you really need. If you can go lower than that - even better. But unfortunately it is often the case that good, light, hiking gear costs more than good and not so light hiking gear.

# More Tips for Pilgrims

## When cheap becomes expensive

Cheap doesn't always mean worse and expensive doesn't always mean good quality, but sometimes cheap can become very expensive, long term. For example, if you buy a cheap backpack only to discover later on that it doesn't fit you, that it rubs your shoulders raw, overburdens your back and in the end breaks when the straps give way, then it can become expensive to replace in the middle of your Camino.

There are lots of ways to save money, for example on your travel costs or your clothes, but try to avoid going down the super cheap route with essential gear like your backpack and boots. A better way to save money on these, without the need to compromise on quality, is to start shopping around early on and to look for end of line/season sales. These models sold might be not exactly the latest fashion in colour, but their functionality will usually be the same as those of newer models.

## Electronics, power outlets, and voltage

Spain's electric voltage is 230 V/50 Hz with the majority of plugs / outlets being either the unearthed two pin "Europlug" or the earthed two pin "Schuko-plug". If you want to use electronics of any kind on the Camino, you will most likely need a travel adapter and if your "home voltage" differs from the voltage in Spain, you will also need a power transformer to put between the power source and your device, to avoid the stronger European voltage frying, for example, your cell phone!

## Environmental issues

Unfortunately you can see a lot of rubbish littering the Camino especially in summer. Suffice it to say that after you having finished eating, take the respective packaging with you to the next garbage bin. It even weighs less without its contents! If you want to do even more, you can take an empty plastic bag with you and collect some additional rubbish that others have left behind and dispose of it in the next village. If more pilgrims would do this, the Camino would soon be as clean as it used to be.

## Bathrooms/ Toilets and NO Outhouses

You usually pass through a village with a bar every 5 to 10 kilometres which for many pilgrims will be every 1.5 to 3 hours. If you aren't near a bathroom and you need a bathroom, please observe the "don't leave anything" rule which means bury your waste, and take the used toilet paper away with you. A small plastic ziplock bag is good to have with you in case of such an emergency (as is a small toilet paper supply). The Camino is currently littered with places sporting toilet paper left by pilgrims and it is a sad thing to see.

## Reading about other pilgrims' experiences

This is one thing that I don't recommend as preparation for your first Camino. It is true that many pilgrims first heard about the Camino de Santiago from the books of Paulo Cuelho, Shirley MacLaine or others. But if you orientate yourself too much on what others have experienced during their pilgrimages, you run the risk of orientating your own expectations about your own Camino on these experiences. You might hope that your own Camino will be like that of Shirley MacLaine, Paulo Cuelho or another author you have read. But in fact you want to experience your own, very personal Camino and not that of others. Correct?

On the other hand, reading non-fiction books about the history, art, culture, etc of the Camino de Santiago is highly recommended. The more you know about the background and history of the country you walk through, the more you will enjoy your own Camino. And learning to speak Spanish is a great way of preparing yourself for this experience of a lifetime.

## Luggage Transport

There are now plenty of companies that offer to transport a pilgrim's luggage from *refugio* to *refugio*. Here are my thoughts regarding this:

Those who send their luggage ahead and carry only a small day-pack count, technically, as a pilgrim with accompanying vehicle and they are the last in the "pecking order" when it comes to the distribution of beds, if there are any left, in the *refugios*. The only exception to this is with some private *refugios* where you can reserve a bed in advance (see below) and obviously hostels, pensions, and hotels.

Unfortunately, some pilgrims pick up their backpack a few hundred meters before the *refugio* and pretend that they have carried it the whole day. Those who plan to do this should consider the following:

The bed that you now occupy has thus been taken away from a pilgrim that has carried a heavy backpack, sweating up and downhill the whole day and is arriving later than you because of this.

Other pilgrims will notice that, while they met you on the way with a small day-pack, you are now arriving with a much heavier one and occupying a bed - not something that will make you many friends amongst other pilgrims!

Part of the Camino experience is to test one's own limits, to expand them and to rejoice when you have accomplished something that you thought originally might be impossible for you.

The offer of luggage transport tempts most people to overload their packs which runs contrary to the idea of letting go of things and to concentrate on and discover the really essential things in your life.

The spontaneity on the Way can easily be lost by such an over-organized approach. Just imagine that you found a nice village and cozy *refugio* where you would love to stay the night - but your backpack is waiting for you somewhere else, in another village, several kilometres / miles further on …

Those, on the other hand, who cannot carry a backpack for health reasons, welcome the availability of a luggage transport which can make the difference between being able to walk the Camino or having to stay home. No doubt that in such cases, luggage transport is a blessing and nobody should frown upon it.

### ***Pilgrim Anecdote***

*The mother of a friend of mine made her pilgrimage from Sarría to Santiago de Compostela and walked the complete 110 km/70 mi. She managed to walk an average of 5 km/3 mi per day and her luggage was transported by a taxi. The reason? She had just finished her treatment for cancer and wanted to do the pilgrimage to celebrate and to thank God that she was still alive. A real pilgrim? I think YES!*

***

**Summary**: Please remember the following Bible verse, even if you are not a Christian. "Do not judge, or you too will be judged!", before you fall into the temptation of judging the behaviour of other pilgrims. You will rarely know the story behind their situation …

### Reservations

Many private *refugios* now offer the possibility to reserve a bed by phone, but you will usually need to be able to speak

Spanish to do so. Is it worth the exchange of spontaneity on the way for the security of a bed? Only you can decide for yourself!

**Safety on the Way**

It seems to be nearly obligatory that everybody that publishes anything about their Camino includes at least one attack by the, oh so dangerous, wild Spanish dogs. Paulo Cuelho started this fashion, Shirley MacLaine continued it and even the German comedian Hape Kerkeling couldn't give it a pass in his book. At least the latter didn't include demonic dogs in his book ...

My tips about what to do if you really feel threatened by dogs have already been covered at the beginning of this book. Here are a few additional points regarding safety that pilgrims, often completely unnecessarily, are concerned about:

**So, how safe is the Camino really? Do pilgrims have to be worried, especially the female ones, to walk it alone?**

**A reality check**: In 2012 the pilgrim's office in Santiago welcomed more than 190,000 pilgrims, who did the pilgrimage on foot, by bike, with a horse/donkey and even in a wheel chair, and arrived safe and sound in Santiago.

From my own experience, both as a pilgrim as well as a *hospitalera*, and from many conversations I have had over the years with other pilgrims and *hospitaleros*, I have gained the impression that the crime rate on the Camino itself is far lower than in any home town of many of the pilgrims. Or, to put it differently, to walk the Camino is less dangerous than, for example, a walk through Chicago. All this being said and put in context, what are the main dangers during your pilgrimage and how can you prevent most of them from happening?

**Important: The emergency phone number in Spain is 112. If something does happen, please don't hesitate to call them. Chances are very good that you will get connected to somebody that speaks English!**

**The English language police hotline for non-emergencies can be found at 902 102 112 and is manned from 09:00h to 21:00h.**

## Wild Animals

Theoretically there are poisonous snakes, scorpions, wolves, and bears in Spain. Practically I haven't met one single pilgrim that has had an unpleasant encounter with one of the first two or has even seen the last two. In the Spanish news over the last few years I have found only one case of a pilgrim that was bitten by a snake and had to spend a few days in hospital. In that case, said pilgrim stepped directly on the snake (I think in sandals) which the reptile, understandably, didn't appreciate, and reacted by biting the pilgrim out of self-defence. **Danger potential**: Very close to zero, just take care of whom you step on and don't reach into stone cairns or similar.

## Illness

An old saying goes "Life is always life threatening and ends in death." For the healthy pilgrim the Camino doesn't pose any special health risk. The mortality rate on the Camino is one to two dozen deaths annually which is certainly below the statistical average of the respective home countries of the pilgrims. And please put this also in perspective in relation to the actual number of pilgrims on the Way each year.

The main causes of the deaths that have been reported on the Camino were traffic accidents, especially when the pilgrims were tired and less attentive and tried to cross the road without looking - or were looking in the wrong direction when coming from a country that drives on the left side of the road - and heart attacks, mainly caused by heat, over-exercising, and pre-existing heart conditions. If you don't feel well, simply stop walking and if things don't get better very soon, take a rest day. If in doubt, see a doctor or call **112**. This is also valid if you notice that another pilgrim is not feeling well. There is no punishment in Spain for calling an ambulance out of serious concern for somebody else, even if that person turns out to not be seriously ill.

## Weather

The weather in the mountains can change incredibly fast and therefore you should always, especially from autumn to spring, listen to the advice of the locals. To cross the Pyrenees from St. Jean Pied-de-Port to Roncesvalles in winter and on the mountain route is, for example, not advisable and has been the cause of death of several pilgrims over the years. Yes, the initial plot in the movie <u>The Way</u> has indeed occurred on the Camino!

### Forest fires

Forest fires are unfortunately frequent in Spain, but they normally don't threaten pilgrims. I have included them here only to remind the smokers to be careful with their cigarettes and ashes - especially in the dry season! So, please don't smoke where the ground is bone dry ...

### Theft

A big lock or a pacsafe© on your backpack signals to potential thieves that "something inside is worth stealing". Plus it adds to the overall weight of the pack. Most of the time a thief will not bother with the lock, but slit your backpack with a knife, only to find your dirty socks inside. Result: Backpack damaged and nothing stolen.

Always take your valuables with you, even if you just go to the toilet or take a shower, in a waterproof bag / money-belt. If you walk in a group, or have made friends with other pilgrims, you can take turns showering while the others keep an eye on the belongings.

Take care that your gear doesn't look expensive, where possible, by replacing the branded camera strap with a more neutral one or by putting a sticker over the Apple logo of your iphone.

Cell phones and all other electronics should be kept in sight when charging them especially if you have passwords saved on them. **Extra tip**: Every time you go to a bar or restaurant choose a table or chair close to a power outlet, this way you can charge your electronics while you eat or drink and you don't need to waste time later watching them in the *refugio*.

During the night, keep valuables in the end of your sleeping bag. Don't open it completely, but rather form a pocket around your feet - just remember not to leave them there if you get up in the night. I actually sleep with my money belt on and with my waist bag, containing my camera and cell phone, in my sleeping bag with me.

Security photocopies of all important papers (passport and travel documents) should be buried deep in your backpack, preferably close to your smelliest socks.

**Extra Tip**: If you have forgotten your charger in the last *refugio*, don't panic. Simply tell the *hospitalero* in the next *albergue*. Most likely, he will hand you a whole box full of forgotten chargers where you, hopefully, can find a good replacement.

**Summary**: Yes, theft does happen, but you shouldn't worry too much about it. Most of the "thefts" are more often misplaced, lost, or rolled under the bed items. It is more dangerous when you venture outside the *refugio* or away from the Camino than it is in the *refugio*. The park around the old refuge in Burgos was notorious for petty theft. Railway and bus stations frequented during your travel to and from the Camino require extra caution.

Common sense (did I mention that this is the least common of all senses around?), average carefulness, and awareness of your surroundings, are the best security measures. Keep in mind that your home town and the travel to / from it to the Camino might well be more dangerous than walking the Camino itself or sleeping in its *refugios*.

**Camino Foxes**

No, not the four-legged variety with the nice red coat: the two-legged, less sympathetic ones. Camino fox is the nickname given by the Spaniards to those people that disguise themselves as pilgrims and try to take financial advantage of other pilgrims from this disguise. (Note that the number of Camino foxes is, compared to the absolute number of pilgrims, extremely low!)

Again, let common sense prevail and, for example, never show anybody where you store your main supply of cash or your bank cards. If you meet a pilgrim that complains that the ATM machine has "eaten" their bank card (which does happen!), invite him for a meal or pay for his stay in the *refugio* instead of lending him the money until he "gets his card back".

## Exhibitionists/molesting of female pilgrims

There are indeed occasional reports about exhibitionists / streakers /flashers on the Camino - very occasional ones! The best course of action if something like this happens to you is to ignore that person completely and just walk past, or, if that is too much for you to bear, walk back and wait for other pilgrims and continue on in a group. Obviously each such case should be reported immediately to the police. Once again **112** is your friend. Oh, and if you happen to have a camera with you, don't hesitate to raise it and snap a pic of the offender if you feel safe to do so. The police will be grateful for such evidence!

**Summary**: After 6000 kilometres / 3700 miles on European pilgrimage routes, half of this in Spain and nearly always as a solo woman, none of the above has ever happened to me. So please don't drive yourself crazy with remote possibilities that are more likely, statistically, to happen in your home town than on the Camino Francés in Spain.

Now that you know all that I know about everyday pilgrim life and its different aspects and have decided when you want to walk and on which route, it is time to look, item by item, at the necessary gear!

## Your Gear

What every pilgrims really needs, what some pilgrims might need, and what, in nearly all cases, can stay at home. These items are set out here in that order. Two annotations ahead:

**Weight**: This indicates the upper limit of weight which a specific piece of gear shouldn't surpass. I don't note this every single time if little difference exists between the typical weight of two items, for example, two different editions of a pilgrim's passport (*credencial*). I therefore mention this only if it means a real difference in weight.

**Specific products and makes**: Apart from a few exceptions, I don't recommend any specific products and brands, instead I explain which points are important to consider when buying a specific piece of equipment and which ones are less important. This way, I aim to aid you in finding the right product that fits your unique needs instead of encouraging you to chase after a certain, fashionable trend.

## What Every Pilgrim Needs

## Weightless Items

The planning for and anticipation of the pilgrimage is nearly as good as the travel itself! If this planning and preparation helps to improve your own pilgrimage experience, so much the better. Here are a few things you can do beforehand to make this happen.

### A visit to your doctor and dentist

A visit to your dentist, especially if some time has passed since your last visit, is always a good idea! Imagine if an unknown cavity in a tooth decides to play up during your pilgrimage. Dentists in Spain are of the same high level of professionalism as your dentist at home, but they rarely speak English and you will, most of the time, have to pay them cash and then try later to get your money back from your insurance, if it covers dental treatment at all. The paperwork with the insurance company can be a lot of hassle and time consuming. A simple pre-camino dentist visit, and treatment if necessary, before you start travelling, can help avoid problems.

The same can be said for a visit to your doctor, especially if you are over 50 and / or suffer from a chronic illness or ailment. For the latter case, it is important to discuss with your doctor how you can handle your specific health situation on the Camino in the best manner possible and how you can prevent possible problems. Without going into too much detail here, every year many people with a chronic illness walk the Camino without any problems.

## First Aid Course

When did you last take a first aid course? Are you sure you still remember how to put somebody in the recovery position? Or how to do CPR in a real emergency situation? A first aid course doesn't cost much but can save a life. It can also save you unnecessary problems if you know how to correctly treat minor injuries on yourself and don't have to rely on others. To find the next first aid course in your home town, just ask at the Red Cross office or a similar organization.

## Knowledge of Spanish and other languages

Spanish is the language all the people that live alongside the Camino will speak, and is obviously the language all Spanish pilgrims (the biggest group) will speak. But the common language amongst the pilgrims is often English! So, this is good news for you! Other languages you will hear frequently are German, Italian, Portuguese and French. The best and cheapest method to improve your own language skills is to find a native speaker that wants to improve his English in exchange for you improving your Spanish. Also many community colleges, or, in the UK, the Open University, offer low cost language courses.

## Physical Preparation

To walk as a pilgrim to Santiago is no mean feat. It means carrying your backpack every single day over many kilometres, uphill and downhill. Those who have never done something like this before are in for a surprise and might often perceive the first few days as "hell". Physical preparation helps to build up muscles, stretch tendons and ligaments, and also allows you to break in your hiking boots and to test your equipment. Start slowly and with a light backpack and increase your exercise gradually until you can carry your fully loaded bag over 20 to 25 km / 12 to 16 mi without feeling too much discomfort.

**Extra tip**: Train your digestive track. Many pilgrims scream "food poisoning" when it is, in reality, just the consequences of a sudden change of diet. The Spanish cuisine is rich in olive oil, and the Galician one is rich in pork fat and many pilgrim's tummies find that too hard to stomach (pun intended) during the first few days. Get a Spanish cookbook or search the internet for recipes or, alternatively, visit your local Spanish restaurant from time to time. This will help you to adapt faster.

And don't forget to also train your skin! A good method to avoid sunburns is to expose your skin to the sun at home before you leave (if this is possible!) and then to protect it with sunscreen / block / long sleeved clothes whilst walking under the hot Spanish sun.


## Pilgrim's Blessing

The Camino traditionally started at home from your own front door. In the past, before trains, buses and aeroplanes were invented, this meant that pilgrims literally started at home and then walked back home again; or took a carriage or a ship, rode a horse, or walked with a donkey, to Santiago and back. Granted, all this would prove rather difficult for most overseas pilgrims, apart from the ship option. Nevertheless, each pilgrimage began with the blessing by the parish priest. Nowadays, only a few pilgrims have the time and money to start from their own door step - and for overseas pilgrims that is rarely feasible. But a pilgrim's blessing is widely available and you don't even have to be a Roman-Catholic to receive one. Simply ask your local parish or St James confraternity if they offer one. Addresses for the latter and the text of a traditional pilgrim's blessing are in the appendix to this book.

And what if you are not a Christian? Do not fear, everybody is allowed to walk the Camino de Santiago without restriction of religion or denomination. You don't need to confess a particular faith to walk the Camino! Non-Christians, please feel free to develop your own departure ritual, be it a goodbye party among friends, or a blessing given by parents, relatives, or close friends. You really can develop your own ritual for your own departure towards the Camino!

## Best Camino Guides

A Camino guide is the first piece of equipment that should be bought as soon as you have decided which way to walk! At the time of writing (April 2013) there are really only two recommended options. One is the yearly updated guide by the Confraternity of St. James (London, UK) which has good route descriptions and exhaustive descriptions of facilities (*refugios*, shops etc.) but not much in terms of maps or height profiles.

It can be found at http://www.csj.org.uk (click "Bookshop" in the top menu). The new edition is always published in January, so bear that in mind when ordering to ensure that you always get the most up to date guide possible.

The other one is "A Pilgrim's Guide to the Camino de Santiago: St. Jean * Roncesvalles * Santiago (Camino Guides)" by John Brierley, which is also very accurate and is regularly updated. It is heavier than the Camino guide by the Confraternity of St. James, but contains maps and contour guides.

**Summary**: If weight is a major concern and you are happy without maps, the Confraternity guide will be your best choice. If, on the other hand, you don't mind carrying a bit more in exchange for detailed maps and contour guides, the guide by John Brierley will be a good fit for you.

Note that both John Brierley and PiliPala Press publish a Camino Map book which could be a good complement to the Confraternity guide. Again, look when they were published / last updated and what scale is used for the maps.

In case you can't find the guides mentioned above, or prefer another author, here are the key points every Camino guide must cover:

It has to be up-to-date which means its publication date (make sure it is a revised edition, not just a re-print) should be as close to the date of your own pilgrimage as possible. The situation on the Camino, especially regarding *refugios*, changes often and permanently.

While the way marking (yellow arrows and shells) is extremely good on the Camino Francés, maps, height profiles, and the route descriptions do help you in planning the next stage. Believe me there is a difference in walking a mile/kilometre up a steep uphill versus over flat terrain!

Most importantly, your guide book should warn you of long stretches without water, ATMs or shops that lie ahead to avoid being stuck on a long deserted patch of the Way without enough water, money and food.

I also prefer a guide book that simply states the amenities in each town/village on the way, but doesn't try to prescribe the pilgrim "daily stages". This way you can decide if you want to walk a bit more to the next village or not, and you can also avoid walking "with the masses".

**Extra Tips**: If your chosen guide is also available as a Kindle edition and you have a modern cell phone, you can download the free Kindle App for your phone and read the guide on it. This will save some weight. In the appendix you'll find some links to freely downloadable documents that list refuges and villages on the Camino.

If you walk with a printed edition, remove (again cut, not rip out) those pages you won't need. This might hurt a bibliophile's heart, but it does reduce the weight in your backpack. Pages you can do without are those about the flora and fauna on the way, stages you have already walked, etc.

**Number**: Obviously only one! That said, one time I met an Austrian pilgrim who had four different guide books with him but nevertheless, or perhaps because of this, got continuously lost.

**Weight**: A print book shouldn't weigh more than 200g. An electronic version is obviously weightless.

**Paperwork**

**Pilgrim Passport (*Credencial*)**

First of all let's look at what a Pilgrim Passport (*credencial* in Spanish) actually is, what you can and can't do with it, and what the prerequisites for getting one are. The *credencial* is issued by the Cathedral in Santiago and by accredited Pilgrims Associations and then distributed amongst the pilgrims in their home countries via said associations. In Spain, they are available in *refugios*, Pilgrim's association offices, and some churches. And no, you don't have to be baptized nor be a Christian in order to get one. The Camino is accessible to everybody, no matter your personal creed. The only prerequisite that you need to fulfil is that you do the pilgrimage either by foot, bike, horseback, or in a wheelchair. Pilgrims that exclusively use a car or the bus are not entitled to one.

Yes, you can get a *credencial* in Spain, but it is advisable to bring one with you as that saves time and hassle. In the appendix you will find the addresses of the English (and one French) speaking pilgrim's associations that issue this document.

The *credencial* also allows you to sleep in designated pilgrim *refugios* which are not open to non-pilgrims, but only if there is a bed/space for you. These *refugios* cost either a small fee, between 3 and 12 Euros, or work on a donation basis.

**Two important points**: First, the beds in these pilgrim refuges are, at least theoretically, for the most tired of pilgrims. Practically that means that pilgrims on foot that carry their own backpack have priority before all others. Thus the pecking order for the beds looks like this and is often organized by time of arrival, i.e. many refuges state that they don't except cyclists before a certain time and pilgrims with an accompanying vehicle much later.

1. Any ill pilgrim, no matter the mode of transport

2. Pilgrim on foot and with backpack

3. Pilgrim with bike, horse, donkey, etc.

4. Pilgrim with luggage transported by a vehicle no matter the mode of transport

Please note that the *credencial* doesn't give you the "right" to a bed. If there aren't any left, the *hospitaleros* might offer you a soft piece of floor or point you to some alternative accommodation, such as a sports hall or even a church. Alternatively, there are usually always other forms of accommodation such as hotels and pensions in nearly all villages and towns on the Camino.

The *credencial* not only allows you to sleep in the designated pilgrim accommodation, it also serves as proof that you really have walked or rode the Camino and can, full of pride, apply in Santiago for a *Compostela*. This proof works via the *sellos*/stamps you collect in your *credential*, (at least one per day at the beginning and later, see below, at least two per day), that are given at *refugios*, churches, pensions, hotels, and bars along the way and are a witness of your passing through the different towns and villages on the Camino.

To get the *Compostela* (a document issued by the Pilgrim's Office in Santiago on behalf of the Cathedral that confirms that you have **completed the pilgrimage for pious reasons**) you will need to heed the following rules:

You need to have walked the **last** 100 kilometres or cycled / rode the **last** 200 kilometres. The "**last**" bit is important, as this is a pilgrimage to a certain place, to the tomb of the apostle St. James in the cathedral of Santiago de Compostela. Walking one hundred kilometres somewhere on the Camino, but not arriving in Santiago under your own steam, will not get you this document that confirms your completed pilgrimage to Santiago.

You need at least one stamp per day, usually done automatically in the *refugio* where you sleep AND two stamps per day for the last 100 kilometres (walkers) or 200 kilometres (riders and bikers) as proof that you really did the Camino and didn't just pass by in a car and collect stamps. As a rule of thumb, this is more closely checked and scrutinized the nearer to Santiago your starting point is. If you started at home, for example in Canterbury (UK) several months ago, everybody in the pilgrim's office will be in such awe that they will hardly give your stamps a second look!

You need to state that you are doing your pilgrimage for religious or spiritual reasons. If you state your reasons as being sportive or cultural you will receive a different document. As the *Compostela* is a Church document that confirms that you have done your pilgrimage out of piety, this rule is understandable if you think about it. In the appendix you can find the text of the *Compostela*, in Latin as it is on the document, and then translated in to English, together with the Spanish and English text of the alternative certificate.

When you have acquired your *Compostela*, you can also eat breakfast, lunch, and dinner for 3 days for free at the *Parador* (Hotel) in Santiago de Compostela. But don't get all excited. You will not eat in the main, posh restaurant, but in a small room adjacent to the kitchen. This offer stems from the fact that this *Parador* was a pilgrim's *refugio* in medieval times. The offer is limited to the first ten pilgrims that show up each day. The Pilgrim's Office in Santiago will help you to locate it if you are interested.

**Other things you can do with your Credencial:** Some museums, churches, and other venues along the Way, that require you to pay an entrance fee, will give pilgrims a discount.

Yes, you can get a *credencial* on arrival in Spain, but you really should save yourself the stress of having to find the place that issues them in the town where you arrive and instead, bring one from home. Addresses of different pilgrim's associations that issue them can be found in the appendix. Please apply for one in good time as the office is typically run by volunteers with limited spare time and from application to having your *credencial* in your own hands, can easily take 4 to 6 weeks, or even more.

If you end up needing to get a *credencial* in Spain, you can usually find one in all major starting points of the Camino, as well as in the bigger towns and *refugios* along the way.

If you want to be absolutely sure that you can get your *credencial* in Spain, you might want to bring a letter of recommendation from your local parish priest. Unfortunately the Camino is getting seen more and more as a way of having a cheap vacation and some of the Spanish pilgrim's associations want to see some sort of proof that you really are a pilgrim and not just a tourist before they issue you a *credencial*. A sample text for such a letter of recommendation, in Spanish, can be also found in the appendix.

**Number**: One. If you run out of space for your *sellos* (stamps), you can find an additional *credencial* in Spain or you can simply insert a blank piece of paper in your existing *credencial* until you can get another one.

## Visa and Passport

### Visa

Citizens of most English-speaking countries don't need a visa for Spain unless they plan to stay more than 90 days in Spain and/or in another country of the European Union (Schengen Area). Whether you need a visa or not depends on a) your nationality and b) how long you plan to stay. At the time of writing (2013), citizens of the following countries didn't need a visa to enter Spain as long as they don't stay more than 90 days: USA, Canada, Australia, and New Zealand. They simply get their passports stamped when they arrive and are required to leave the Schengen area before their 90 days are up. Citizens of a European Union country (Schengen) obviously don't need a visa at all and can stay longer than 90 days in Spain. Citizens of South Africa do require a visa that has been issued before travelling to Europe.

As visa regulations change frequently, please check with the Spanish embassy in your home country or country of residence to see what applies to you. Again, the respective addresses can be found in the appendix of this book.

### Passport

Everybody needs a valid passport. The official position in Spain is that your passport has to only be valid for the time you are in Spain. Nevertheless it is a good idea to make sure that its validity extends 6 months past your return home date in case you fall into the hands of an over-eager customs officer or you are planning a stop-over in another country on your way home.

Apart from the original documents of passport and visa, if applicable, it is also a good idea to make copies of these documents and store them separately. If you want to be extra careful you can also make a digital copy (photo or scan) and upload that into the "cyber cloud" by sending it as an attachment to your own email address.

**Number**: Originals and paper copies plus a digital copy in the "cyber cloud".

## Health and Travel Insurance

Not so long ago ill and injured pilgrims were treated for free in Spain, but with the revival and popularity of the pilgrimage that has stopped. Therefore you absolutely need to carry valid travel health insurance. What you need and don't need depends, again, on where you come from.

## EU Citizens - European Health Insurance Card (EHIC)

If you are a citizen of any of the 27 EU countries or of Iceland, Liechtenstein, Norway, or Switzerland, the absolute minimum you need to bring is a valid European Health Insurance Card (EHIC). With this you are treated, if ill or injured, like any Spanish citizen would be treated and under the same conditions. That means you will be treated for free by doctors and in hospitals that are part of the public health care system. It is common for doctors and hospitals to treat private patients and public health care patients at the same time and location, so make sure that they understand that you are looking for free public health care by showing them your EHI Card. Public health care in Spain is excellent and of a very high standard. You will need to pay upfront for private health care which is not refundable under the EHIC system though it may be refundable by a private health/travel insurance depending on what policy you bought.

## Treatment generally covered with an EHIC

All treatment, including diagnostics, in a public hospital, emergency room, and health centre.

## Treatment generally NOT covered with an EHIC

Dental treatment.

Treatment as a private patient in hospitals, etc.

Transport back to your home country.

## Prescriptions

Unless you are a pensioner, and can prove it, you will be charged a percentage of your prescription cost, some of which might be refundable later on in your home country - so keep receipts!

## EU Citizens - Additional Travel Health Insurance

Even if the EHIC system covers you in case of sudden illness and injury, it might be a good idea to have an additional travel and health insurance policy. There are innumerable policy options out there. Here a few tips to get you started with your research:

Ask any insurance provider that you already use if they also offer travel health insurance. This way you already know something about their level of service.

Make sure that your chosen insurance includes walking/hiking vacations and doesn't put it under "dangerous and not covered activities".

Ask how things work in case of an emergency. Do they have a 24/7 telephone number? Will they pay the doctor and hospital directly? Will they provide you, if necessary, with an interpreter? Does the policy include your transportation back to your home country? Which, if any, of your pre-existing conditions are excluded from coverage?

Chances are good that you will never need this, but if you do need it, having it will save you a lot of money and worry.

## Non-EU Citizens

Basically what I wrote in the paragraph just above this one, regarding additional travel health insurance, applies to you also, only in your case this will be your main insurance and not an additional one. Choose wisely and read the small print carefully. Don't even think of travelling to Europe without health insurance in the hope that your embassy will bail you out of the hospital bills! They will do so initially, but you will need to pay every single cent back to them! Make sure that you have sufficient health insurance coverage before leaving home as a broken ankle or similar, could leave you with a lot of debt if you don't have travel health insurance.

**Extra Tips**: South African citizens need to check that their health insurance maximum coverage is high enough, as you have to have proof of this when applying for a visa!

Canadians should avoid flying via the USA to Europe as this increases the cost of travel health insurance. Strange, but true ...

**Number**: Original policies plus photocopies. Don't forget to record the contact number of your insurance company where you can find it. I keep it in my money belt or you could save it in your phone. In an emergency, the last thing you want to do is try to find the contact number amongst a bunch of papers whilst being in pain because of a sprained ankle ...

## Travel tickets

Depending on how you plan your travel to the Camino and back home, you will have several papers for your travel bookings. Make sure you know if you need to confirm any of these a few days before your departure and make a note of this and the telephone number you need to call.

**Number**: Travel tickets plus copies.

## Other papers to bring

If you plan to rent a car in Santiago, you will obviously need to bring your driving license if you are an EU citizen, or an International Driving Permit plus your local driving license, if you are not.

If you plan to send postcards to your nearest and dearest you will need to take their respective addresses with you, either on paper or electronically.

If you are a student, don't forget to bring your ISIC card to get reductions on entrance fees to exhibitions and museums, plus reduced travel costs after Santiago.

And last but not least, you will need a list of your relevant emergency numbers to, for example, get a lost/stolen credit card blocked. Equally important are your log-in details for your email account, online banking, and so on. These obviously, should be kept extremely safe and disguised.

**Number**: Try to combine as many of your papers as possible or save everything possible into your cell phone and/or in your email account/cyber cloud.

**Extra Tip**: A cell phone that contains this important information should be protected by a strong password and never left unattended!

### Keeping your documents safe and dry

All these important documents have to be kept safe and dry (rain and sweat!) and be carried theft-proof under your clothes. A good way to achieve this is to use a water and sweat proof bag or money belt worn under your clothes. It is best to wear it around your neck or around your waist as a holster-style security pouch will interfere with your backpack straps and soon become uncomfortable. Second copies, in plastic document covers, should be buried deep in your backpack close to the least appealing part of your luggage - smelly socks ...

**Number**: One waterproof bag or money belt that can be carried around your neck or waist plus a few plastic document covers.

### Money and Budget

Though going on a pilgrimage isn't expensive, some budgeting has to be done. As for me, long live the Euro! The first time I walked the Camino, each European country still had its own currency: the Franc in France and the Peseta in Spain. Nowadays travel in Europe has become considerably easier currency wise.

You should always carry enough cash to cover the expenses of the next two or three days plus your ATM cards (and either the pins in your memory or hidden well in your money belt). Spanish cash-points/ATM (Automatic Teller Machines) accept all the usual debit and credit cards, like Visa and Mastercard, as long as they have a numerical 4-digit security PIN enabled. Note that I wrote **numerical 4-digit PIN code** as 6-digit codes are not accepted in Europe and if you don't know the equivalent of your letters in numbers, you will quickly run into problems. If you are not sure if your card will work in

Europe, please ask your bank about this before setting off! American Express is NOT widely accepted in Europe. You can use it at cash-points/ATMs but you will have problems using it to pay for bigger bills in hotels, etc.

While ATM machines are widely available in the towns on the Camino, only bigger and really upmarket places will accept anything other than cash so make sure you carry enough cash with you as an average Spanish shopkeeper will shake his head when he sees your cards!

It is also wise to carry at least two different cards as Spanish ATMs are known for "swallowing" cards, if, for example, you mistyped your PIN too often. Until you can get your card back when the bank opens the next day (or the day after if it is a weekend) you will need to "survive" and so carrying a second card is wise.

**Important Tips:**

Budget so that you don't need to take cash out at a "hole in the wall" on a Friday afternoon or a weekend! This way you only have to wait until the next morning to get your swallowed card back, if that should happen.

Arrive with 200 or 300 Euros cash so that you don't have to deal with cash machines immediately in a new country.

Traveller's cheques are rarely used anymore in Europe and are pretty much a thing of the past - Cash and plastic reign on the Camino!

Inform your bank that you plan to travel abroad: you don't want to get your card(s) blocked as a security measure because of suspected "suspicious activity".

Ask beforehand what the costs are for each withdrawal of money from an ATM and if there are differences in these fees depending on which bank you choose to withdraw your money. This way you can save a few dollars by ideally only using partner banks of your bank and by withdrawing the maximum amount for the lowest applicable fee.

**Budget:** Living a simple pilgrim's life - always staying in non-private *refugios*, having picnics on the side of the way, and not eating out nor indulging in *café con leche* and similar in a local bar - can keep daily costs at around 20 Euro or even less. A budget of 25 Euros/day allows for the occasional pilgrim's menu or other treats in local bars and restaurants. If you have more "daily allowance" you can either treat yourself to a hotel from time to time or leave an extra large donation in one of the *refugios* that depend on it for taking care of all pilgrims, no matter if they have little, none, or a lot of money.

**Amount**: Enough cash for a few days, depending on your budgeting and two debit or credit cards plus the necessary telephone numbers to block them, stored in a different location!

**Important**: The maximum withdrawal at an ATM is normally 300 Euro / day and you will get charged a fee for every single one, the height of which depends on your bank. So avoid, if possible, to withdraw smaller amounts too frequently!

## Wallet

While cards, passport, and larger amounts of cash belong in your money belt/pouch, you will still need a small wallet for everyday purchases. Some pilgrims prefer to use a "kangaroo-style" belt pouch that is big enough for some additional items like a notebook, pen, cell phone, a snack or two, and your daily money. Others simply carry a light weight, small wallet somewhere easily accessible in their backpack. I have already mentioned that carrying your wallet in your back pocket is a really stupid idea - haven't I?

**Number**: One, the smaller and lighter the better, or a bigger belt pouch in which you can keep handy all that you might need during the day.

## The Ideal Pilgrims' Backpack

The backpack is, together with the boots (see below), the most important piece of gear for the pilgrim. It should be comfortable to carry, light, neither too big nor too small, and allow you to organize your belongings. Upholstered shoulder straps and hip belt as well as good ventilation for your back are equally important. The most important thing is to choose the backpack personally and to try it on, fully loaded, before buying it. A good Outdoor shop will understand and facilitate this.

The size of a backpack is measured in litres with 50 litres being a good average size for the Camino. How big a backpack really needs to be depends on two factors - weather and money. Those who plan to make a winter pilgrimage will need more and warmer (thicker and heavier) clothes and sleeping bag. Those who can't afford to buy the best, smallest, and lightest gear will need a bigger backpack because of the bigger volume of a less costly sleeping bag. Note that a bigger backpack also weighs that bit more. Therefore it is best to first buy most of your gear, especially the sleeping bag, and then, when you know exactly how much volume you need, your backpack.

Other points to consider:

- Does the backpack have a built-in rain cover?
- How many compartments and/or pockets are there to organize your belongings?
- There are now different models available for men and women, as women often have a shorter back than men.
- Can you move your head freely if the pack is fully loaded or is it so high that it disturbs your head movement and sight?
- Can you take the top piece off and use it as a day pack?

The latter is especially practical if you want to go shopping or sightseeing, after having arrived in the *refugio* and don't fancy carrying your big pack into town. In case your chosen backpack doesn't have this option, take a very light fabric bag with you and use that.

And finally, you shouldn't underestimate the weight of your chosen backpack when it is empty. One warning: Some books or websites recommend using a lighter, day pack style backpack with a 35 litre volume or even lower and a weight of only one pound (½ kilo). While 35 litres may be enough in summer, especially if you are an experienced ultra-light packer and have the respective gear, an extremely light-weight backpack that weighs only a pound, normally does not have a comfortable, upholstered hip belt and only narrow shoulder straps. A good backpack "carries itself" but for this you need a good, upholstered, adjustable hip belt and shoulder straps otherwise these shoulder straps will cut horribly into your shoulders as the whole weight of your pack rests only on them. The weight you might have saved by buying a lighter backpack will not make up for this pain.

**Number**: One, plus if it doesn't have an integrated day pack, a very light, simple fabric bag for shopping and the like.

**Weight**: a 50 litre pack doesn't have to be heavy, look for a model that weighs less than 2 kg.

## Sleeping Bag

Even in summer, it can get chilly at night on some parts of the Camino. Equally in summer, it is also possible that the *refugios* are so full that the only available sleeping place is in a Church porch. If you are on the Way during low season, and especially in winter, you should know that not all *refugios* have central, or any, heating at all. A good sleeping bag is a must-have for every pilgrim! The only exception: If you know from the beginning that you will only sleep in hotels or pensions and never in a pilgrim's *refugio*.

## What makes a good sleeping bag?

It is warm, can be opened completely to serve as a blanket if you are too warm, is light and can be compressed to take up little space. Unfortunately sleeping bags that fulfil all four conditions are rather expensive. If you find a good, reasonably priced one that fulfils the first three points, consider buying a compression sac to take care of the last point. Make sure the sleeping bag is long enough so that you can stretch out comfortably and are still completely covered and warm.

## Material

Down filled bags offer the best insulation and are light in weight. Their disadvantage is that if they become wet or damp, the down will clump together and their ability to insulate decreases. They are also more expensive than those filled with synthetic fibres. The latter ones are not only cheaper, they also dry faster from sweat or rain and they survive the continuous compressing, packing, and unpacking better. Down bags don't like to be compressed too much as the down can break. To walk the Camino I would choose a good sleeping bag filled with a synthetic material over a down-filled one.

## Comfort Temperature

In the warmer season (May to September), a sleeping bag with a **comfort** temperature of 10 C will be sufficient on most routes. The rest of the year, and especially on the Northern Way, you should opt for one whose comfort temperature is 0 C, or even below.

**Extra Tips**: Make sure that you look at the advertised comfort temperature and not at the minimum temperature (possible survival temperature). In some countries it is also usual to refer to the warmer sleeping bags as "four seasons" or "winter" sleeping bags and to the less warm ones as "three seasons" or "summer" sleeping bags.

## Form

Sleeping bags come in two main forms, mummy or rectangular "blanket-style". During summer the latter is sufficient, but in cold weather/winter a mummy (horrible name, I know!) style bag is preferable as it is closer to the body and you will need to heat up less air around you. Plus they also have a hood which can be practical in really cold *refugios*.

**Bag liners**: The idea behind this is to have an inner sleeping bag that can be easily washed when needed and that dries quickly. That sounds great, but remember that every gram counts! Those who are on the road for only a few weeks can give this luxury a pass, those who are walking for months can think about it if the extra weight is worth it.

**Extra Tip**: The bag (stuff sac) that the sleeping bag is stored in can, when filled with clothes, serve as a pillow at night. This prevents neck and shoulder problems and makes for a better sleep. (There is not necessarily a pillow if you stay in non-private *refugios*.)

**Extra Tip**: Don't try to be too orderly and roll / fold your bag when packing it - it will not work. Instead just start at one corner and stuff it roughly into its bag, close the bag, and then pull the compression straps.

**Number**: One sleeping bag in a bag or compression bag.

**Weight**: A good sleeping bag shouldn't weigh more than 1 kilo and it is better if it weighs less.


## Water Container

I intentionally did not write "water bottle" and surely not "water bag" or "drinking system" as I have a pretty low opinion of them (see below). The best solution is, in my experience, a simple, clear plastic soft drink bottle. Yes, a 1.5 litre Cola bottle is exactly what I mean.

Why not a thermos or insulated bottle? This sounds great initially as drinks stay cool in summer and warm in winter, but seriously, they are far too heavy! I would recommend one of these only to those that plan to walk a full winter Camino. They can be filled in the morning with hot sweet tea or coffee and that helps you to stay warm.

The water bladders that are carried in your backpack and let you drink via a tube during walking are, in my opinion, responsible for a lot of "food poisoning" among pilgrims each year. Whilst the idea is attractive on first thought, they have many disadvantages:

Difficult to clean and therefore a breeding ground for germs - especially if you want to fill them occasionally with something other than pure water.

Difficult to judge how much water you still have left and difficult to refill at the fountain or by the nice bartender.

**Note by the co-author Daphne, that slightly disagrees with me on that point:** Using a water bladder means that I can drink water whenever I want as I am walking and don't need to try to fit a bottle in to the side pocket of my pack nor take it off my back to have a drink. I do agree with Sybille that it is difficult to know how much water you have left, and they are awkward to fill in a bathroom sink or by the nice bartender!

What about light-weight hard plastic bottles then? One word - breakage! While they are light, they do break / get damaged easily with the slightest drop.

## So, what is the best alternative?

As I said above, just buy a 1.5 litre soft drink bottle upon arrival in Spain. They are light, not rigid and therefore less prone to break, and have a safe screw top. They are also easy to (re)fill and clean and, as they are transparent, you can always see how much water you have left. And if needed, they are easily replaceable. If you need more capacity for a long waterless stretch, just buy another bottle of Sprite or similar the evening before and carry it. Your muscles will appreciate the sugar and you have an extra, light-weight water container for the next day.

If you are after something a bit more special, you can build your own light weight insulated thermos bottle. Simply cover the whole bottle, excluding the screw top, with aluminium foil. Do two to three layers of this, make sure that all layers are snug around the bottle body, and then add some layers, 6 to 8 are enough, of newspaper and fix and cover with wide tape.

If you are a budding artist and want to personalize your bottle even further, replace the last newspaper layer with white or coloured paper and decorate it to your heart's content. Now you have your very own, personalized Camino bottle that costs little, weighs even less and provides some insulation for your drinks. Plus you will be the envy of your fellow pilgrims.

The best place to carry your water bottle is in the lower part of your backpack's outside pockets or in your hip belt so that you can reach it without the need to take your backpack off every time. If a 1.5 litre water bottle is too big for that, just carry a 0.5 litre water bottle easily accessible and a 1 litre bottle as back-up.

**Extra Tips**: Water is heavy! There is no reason to fill your water bottle to the top all the time. After a few days you will have developed a feeling for how much water you will most likely need until the next fountain.

A soft drink bottle filled with hot tap water doubles as a hot water bottle at night if the *refugio* is really chilly and your feet are really chilly! Or, if you are a woman, and unlucky, for "that" time of the month ...

**Number**: One 1.5 litre plastic bottle that can easily be bought on arrival in Spain. A second bottle, if necessary, can be bought anywhere when the need arises.

## Body Care
### The Basics

One screw top bottle filled with liquid soap that triples as shower gel, shampoo, and clothes washing soap plus tooth brush, paste, floss, a small comb or brush, sun cream or blocker which can also be used as normal skin cream, and a good foot cream; that is all that you will need. Leave the eye-liner, after-shave, and other fashionable stuff at home!

Everything liquid should be in a screw top bottle, trust me on that. Bottles that you just "snap" open will easily do so in your backpack and if you have ever found an open bottle of shampoo in your belongings you will not want to repeat that experience. Those who fly to/from the Camino should also consider the 100 ml liquid rule airlines have when it comes to your carry on luggage. In general you will need far less soap then you think - a small drop goes a long way. And remember, there are shops in Spain!

Those who have problems with chafing of the skin between the thighs or buttocks, should also carry a small tin of Penaten® or a similar baby cream. A small tube of cortisone cream might also come in handy as this is only available by prescription from a doctor in Spain. Powder in all forms should be left at home. It clumps quickly when wet (sweating!) and that worsens the problem by rubbing/chafing the skin even more.

If you walk with a friend/partner you can obviously share a lot. Having different types of shower gel, for example, for men and women is more of a marketing trick than a necessity of life.

Some pilgrims carry a small deodorant stick or roller. It is a fact that the body is perfectly able to adjust and self-regulate the sweat production after a few days without antiperspirant. Just try it out at home for a few days and remember that every gram that you don't carry makes your pilgrim life easier and let's you sweat less!

**Extra Tips**: If you run out of something and can only find a large bottle of it in Spain, simply share with other pilgrims or leave the rest behind in a *refugio* for the benefit of the pilgrims that follow.

## Cosmetics and Make-Up

### ***Pilgrim Anecdote***

*The same Brazilian pilgrim that I mentioned in the beginning of this book, the one with seven differently coloured rain outfits, also brought an ample supply of cosmetics and make-up with her, including different creams for day and night. That wouldn't have been too bad, but unfortunately she had rather expensive taste and all her cosmetics came in heavy glass vessels with just a drop of cream in the middle ...*

\*\*\*

As already mentioned, a single sun cream or blocker that can also be used as your normal skin cream is completely sufficient. You really don't need make-up on the Camino. It is neither a fashion show nor a catwalk.

**Exception:** medical skin cream and medical make-up for people with a skin disease / problem.

## Nail Scissors or Clippers

Nails grow quickly and should be kept short on the Camino to avoid problems with blisters and chaffing. Nail scissors can also be used for cutting bandages, opening packages, cutting your sewing thread, etc. With a bit of practice you can achieve the same with nail clippers (cutting plaster and bandages to size perhaps excluded).

**Extra Tip**: You can treat yourself before you leave home with a pedicure to get your feet "Camino ready". Be sure to tell him that you will soon start a long-distance walk so that he doesn't remove too much hard skin.

**Number**: Either one pair of nail scissors or one set of nail clippers - not both!

## Razors

Pilgrims that don't want to or can't grow a beard, should think about leaving their electric razor at home and shave the old-fashioned way (or carry a lightweight plastic razor). This means less weight and less hassle with different plugs, power outlets, and voltages.

## Toilet Paper

Half a roll is enough and those who want to save even more weight can take the inner cardboard roll out. Not all *refugios*, bars, and restaurant have toilet paper and when "nature calls" along the Way, you will need it. Toilet paper also doubles as tissue, should you have a cold or hay-fever. Put it in a ziplock plastic bag and carry it in a trouser pocket, in your belt pouch or the outside pocket of your backpack to keep it handy.

**Extra Tip**: When "nature calls" on the Camino between towns, there are no toilets nor outhouses. Please remember to pack out your toilet paper (no trace "camping"). You can carrying an extra ziplock plastic bag for this.

## Boots, Shoes, Sandals or ???

This is another piece of equipment that should be bought as early as possible!

### ***Pilgrim Anecdote***

*I still remember with horror, the group of Italian seminarians that started their own pilgrimage in O' Cebreiro, Galicia and literally only then did they take their boots out of the shoe boxes they had bought them in. Brand new shoes and the next day the poor boys had one of the most difficult descents of the whole way before them. I don't even want to imagine the blisters that they must have had the next evening!*

\*\*\*

## So, which shoes are now the ideal pilgrim shoes?

As with so many other things, the ideal pilgrim shoe depends on the pilgrim. If you know that your ankles need extra support / sprain easily, you need boots that support them adequately. If you don't have any problems with your ankles, you can wear lower boots. If you walk during the colder time of the year or in winter, you will need warmer boots than somebody who walks in the summer heat.

The most frequently used materials are GoreTex® or similar (waterproof and breathable), leather, or a combination of these materials. And don't forget the weight! Unfortunately, the same holds true here that more expensive is often better! I normally don't recommend specific makes and models, but Lowa offers in their Renegade GTX series great shoes that not only I, but also many other pilgrims, are excited about. They are widely available in stores in Europe, but not in some other countries. In that case, you need to look online (Amazon) for them.

Flimsy trainers/running shoes are not adequate for the Camino for several reasons. They are not waterproof, they don't support the ankle at all, and they often have very thin soles with not enough grip/profile.

Equally, heavy (mountain) hiking boots are overkill, especially in summer.

**Extra Tip**: Shoes should always be fitted in the afternoon and ideally after having spent the whole day on your feet, as your feet tend to expand during the day and a shoe that fits perfectly early in the morning might be uncomfortably tight later in the day. Take the socks that you plan to wear on your pilgrimage plus any medical insoles you might need, with you to the store. If in doubt, always choose the slightly larger shoes as your feet will swell on the Camino!

**Number**: One pair of light weight waterproof and breathable walking boots.

**Weight**: Please leave your heavy mountaineering boots at home. Good Camino shoes should weigh between 750-1000g (depending obviously on your shoe size).

**Sandals or Crocs®**

Sandals, or similar, fulfil three purposes for a pilgrim.

- If the weather is nice (no rain), many stages of the Camino can be walked in a pair of good walking / hiking sandals which gives your feet a break from your boots.

- Upon arrival in the *refugio,* they can be put on to allow the feet to rest or can be worn when you walk into town later in the day.

- You can wear then in the shower to keep your feet clean.

If you know that you will not walk in sandals on the Camino (winter/need for ankle support) then you can take ultra-light flip-flops or similar instead. Crocs® might be ideal in winter when you need some insulation under your feet when walking around in the cold *refugios* and they are very lightweight.

If, on the other hand, you know that you will walk some stages of the Camino in sandals, you need to invest in a good pair of walking/hiking sandals, ideally ones with a closed toe cap so that stones have less chance of finding their way in (Keens® are a good, though heavy, option). Look for thick, shock-absorbing soles with a good grip/profile.

## Toe Shoes / Five Finger Shoes

Five Finger® shoes, like the models Vibram® makes, or other similar "barefoot shoes" are a relatively new trend. Simply said, they are like gloves for your feet that allow for a more protected "barefoot" walking. A few pilgrims each year do the Camino exclusively in these. Keep in mind that shoes of this type offer no ankle support whatsoever and only a few really waterproof models exist. You will also need special toe socks to go with them and you will have to get used to a completely different walking style. On the plus side, these shoes are very lightweight and incredibly comfortable once you get used to them. Perhaps they are best in summer as an alternative to the heavier hiking sandals. If you have never walked in this kind of "gloves shoes" with a backpack on your back, you should first try it out during a weekend hike. In all cases, you need to choose a trekking model with thick soles (shock absorption!). In the appendix are some links to relevant websites.

## Going completely barefoot

### ***Pilgrim Anecdote***

*Baudoin came walking from Belgium, in winter and always barefoot! What really surprised me was that while his hands showed some frost damage, his feet were in a perfect state.*

\*\*\*

I must add that I have met more pilgrims that tried to walk the Camino barefoot and then bought themselves shoes than vice versa! If you are thinking about doing a barefoot pilgrimage, consider the following: there is higher risk of injuries through stones, broken glass, and the like, plus no support at all for your ankles. Realistically, only people who regularly walk barefoot and have done so for years should consider doing the Camino this way.

**Number**:

**Summer**: Either a pair of ultra-light flip-flops for *refugio* use only (shower!) OR a pair of good walking/hiking sandals OR Five Finger ® shoes with thick soles for Camino walking and to wear in the *refugio*.

**Winter**: A pair of good hiking sandals, Crocs® OR thick soled Five Finger® shoes for the *refugio* (remember the floors can be cold!) and town / village visits.

**Weight**: Flip-Flops and similar can be found that weigh under 100g, good hiking sandals weigh in at several 100g and Five Finger® shoes are somewhere in the middle.

## Clothing

*\*\*\*Pilgrim Anecdote\*\*\**

*One afternoon while I was doing duty in the refuge in Santo Domingo de la Calzada a neighbour came into the office and asked me if I could help him with his packing list as he was planning to walk the Camino soon. Sure, no problem, with pleasure. And so he started reading from his list:*

*"30 pares de calcetines " (Thirty pairs of socks …)*

*What??? On further investigation and questioning, I discovered that yes, he really meant thirty pairs of socks. And every time a few pairs were dirty he planned to mail them home to his wife. I am sure she would have been thrilled to receive each such parcel! Two hours later we had got a handle on his packing list and saved his marriage!*

\*\*\*

## The Onion Layer System

The Onion Layer System, better known in the English-speaking world as the layered clothing system, is really the best friend of a pilgrim! In spring and fall / autumn, it can be warm enough during the day to walk in a t-shirt and even in summer, especially in the mountains, cold enough in the evenings/at night that you need a jacket or a fleece jumper/sweater. The basic idea of the layer system is to use several thin layers instead of one thick one. This allows you to "fine-tune" the amount of clothes worn to achieve the optimal coziness and protection against the weather. Two or more thin layers will provide more insulation due to the air trapped between them and be lighter than one thick one.

Here is the basic system explained:

Base or first layer: Thin, and especially in winter, close fitting to the body. It's job is to wick moisture/sweat away from the body and keep the skin dry. Synthetic materials (quick dry) or merino wool are the most common materials used for this layer.

Middle or insulating layer: Like the name says, this layer provides the warmth and "receives" the moisture wicked away by the inner layer. Wool or fleece are favourite materials for this one. In really cold weather, this layer can be doubled.

Shell layer: Provides wind and rain/snow protection, often made from Gortex®. There is always a trade-off here between waterproof and breathable, in heavy rain/snow a fourth layer (see below) that is 100% waterproof needs to be added.

**Rain Gear**

Poncho, rain pants/trousers, gaiters – which of these do you really need?

First I would recommend a good rain poncho, made out of strong material that covers yourself and your backpack. If you are on the Camino during a time of the year when rain is less frequent (summer), this will be completely sufficient in my experience.

In spring and autumn rain can fall, especially in Galicia, for days without ceasing. Then gaiters and rain pants/trousers are worth their relatively little weight in gold, as they prevent the rain from entering from the top into your, hopefully waterproof, shoes. Oh, and leave the umbrella at home, rain and wind go most of the time hand in hand on the Camino and render it pretty much useless.

Apart from rainy days, rain gear can come in handy on cold, dry and windy days as a windbreaker, and on snowy days to prevent the snow from settling directly on your clothes and then melting and soaking you.

Why not a rain jacket? The short answer to this question is: Shoulder straps! A rain jacket protects the pilgrim and a separate rain cover is available for the backpack, but neither of the two protects the shoulder straps of your backpack from getting wet, which then in turn can become, if the rain is heavy enough, an entrance for water into your backpack (wick effect).

To avoid a rain poncho becoming too unruly in heavy wind and blowing over your head, use a piece of string as a belt replacement. The same string can later be used in the *refugio* as an emergency clothes line. Remember? Multi-use of your equipment!

**Number**: One good rain poncho made out of strong material that covers pilgrim and backpack in summer and, for the "rain season", add in a pair of waterproof pants and gaiters. Or, even better, waterproof pants with built-in gaiters.


## Socks

The right socks, combined with well broken in shoes, are the best prevention against blisters I know of. I myself use the "two socks system" combined with a good foot cream. First of all I cream my feet thickly (Vaseline®, Neutrogena® or Nivea®, all will work fine). Second I put on a pair of really thin socks, made from bamboo or one of these new "tech" microfibre materials that wick away the moisture from the skin. Third comes a thick pair of hiking socks. Note that all socks are seamless. This way I can ensure that friction, (the main cause of blisters forming), occurs between the two pairs of socks, not between the skin and a sock. The best blisters are those you don't get. Creaming the feet generously leaves the skin soft and elastic and keeps moisture away from it: moisture that would otherwise make your skin more prone to blisters.

Those who prefer the "one pair of socks" method should take care that the socks are thick, fit like a glove, let your skin breath and stay dry, are seamless, and are fast drying. You could also use a pair of high-tech double-layered socks.

The company "1000 miles" offers an interesting warranty for their socks. Quote from their website: "Money back or replacement if, within one year from date of purchase, **either you experience blisters** ..." These socks are sold worldwide and perhaps worth exploring, albeit pretty expensive! Website: http://www.1000mile.co.uk

**Extra Tips**: Many experienced pilgrims and long distance hikers recommend not washing your outer pair of socks too often as the socks take on the form of your feet over time. But please, in this case, keep both socks and shoes out of the dormitories - your fellow pilgrims will thank you for your consideration! Your inner socks should be washed and dried daily. Creaming your feet at least twice a day will be enough to keep your skin soft and elastic.

**Number**: Either three pairs of thin socks and three pairs of thick socks or only three pairs of thick, perhaps double-layered, socks. All of them seamless and anatomically correct (right/left versions).

## Underwear

Your beloved cotton undies don't belong on the Camino! They dry too slowly and don't keep moisture (sweat) away from your body because they don't "wick" it away. So-called quick dry wear is not too expensive, dries faster, and wicks moisture/sweat away from your skin to prevent hypothermia and cramped muscles. Merino wool underwear does the same. An undershirt will only be needed in winter. If you feel chilly from spring to autumn just put on another t-shirt (see below).

**Extra Tips**: When choosing the colour, consider that your underwear could also serve as an emergency swimming/sun bathing outfit.

Women should take a well fitting sports bra with wide straps. Make sure that bra straps and backpack straps go well together and no pressure/friction occurs between them. Razor/X-shaped straps are best.

**Number**: Three pairs of underpants plus, for women, one or two sport bras depending if you want to walk into town "without" whilst your bra is drying on the clothes line. In deepest winter add two warm (ski) long sleeves undershirts as an inner layer (see above under "Onion System").

## Trousers and Skirts

Jeans are too heavy, dry too slowly, and normally do not have enough big pockets. Pilgrims are better served by wearing outdoor or trekking trousers, preferable those where you can zip on/off the legs. These are made of modern fabrics that are light and dry quickly, and they have sufficient zipped pockets for all the little things you want to keep handy like your pocket knife or your Camino guide. Just make sure the zip is below the knee area, if not they tend to chaff your thighs ...

In the warmer season, I walk in capri length trousers and have a pair of long trousers for when I am finished walking for the day.

For women, it might be a good idea, especially in the warmer season, to also take a very lightweight skirt, made out of silk perhaps, or a pareo/sarong for the evenings or the rest days when you might want to indulge yourself in a skirt from time to time.

**Extra Tips**: Spaniards are used to pilgrims and their outfits, nevertheless, they still appreciate it when you enter a Church dressed in longish trousers/skirt and a T-shirt/top that covers the shoulders. Nobody will frown at you when you wear something more sportive/shortish, but many will smile at you when you dress up moderately on these occasions.

If you have trousers with zip on/off legs, you will often not need to wash the whole pair but only the legs. One more task saved.

### ***Pilgrim Anecdote***

*A well beloved sight on the Camino is my Scottish pilgrim friend Hamish, who always walks the Camino in his kilt! The faces of the neighbours, at least in the beginning, were a sight to behold when he turned up. Now they are used to him as he walks the Camino nearly every year in this outfit. Something to think about, especially as he stresses the point that his kilt not only gives him a lot of opportunity to chat with the people that live alongside the way, but also provides some nice ventilation for his "legs" during the hotter time of the year. So why not walk the Camino in your Country's traditional dress? Dare to be different and make the Camino more colourful!*

\*\*\*

**Number**: Two pairs of walking/trekking trousers with removable legs or 1 pair of trousers and 1 pair of capri length trousers and for the women, if you feel like it, a lightweight skirt or pareo.

## T-Shirts

A T-Shirt is an incredible versatile piece of clothing. It can serve as undershirt, nightshirt, and obviously as T-shirt, plus it adds an extra insulation layer in really cold weather. Here again modern fabrics, (quick dry wear) or merino wool, is preferable to cotton. Light colours are better than dark ones as you a) get seen better and b) they reflect a tiny bit more the sun/heat and don't heat up as quickly as, for example, black. In the cooler time of the year or on the Northern Route, one or two of these should have long sleeves. The "daily schedule" of a T-shirt looks like this in my case: Arrive at the *refugio*, wash clothes and pilgrim, put on fresh clothes, enjoy social time, sleep in the same fresh clothes/T-shirt (and in winter even in the same fresh trousers) and start walking the next day in the clothes I slept in. Really, nobody on the Camino cares if your clothes have a "freshly ironed" look or not!

T-shirts for the summer should be bought one to two sizes larger than what you normally wear, so that they don't sit too close to the body but allow for an insulating layer of air between body and clothes. In winter a quick dry or merino wool shirt that fits snugly and keeps your skin dry is better.

Short sleeves means that at least the shoulders, and even better, the upper arms, are still covered. This protects from sunburn - I don't recommend walking in a tank top. Those who have had sunburn on their shoulders and/or upper arms and then tried putting on a backpack, know why I recommend not wearing one! Ensure that the short sleeve length on your T-shirts is long enough to cover your upper arms to protect you from the backpack's shoulder straps rubbing your inner arms raw. This is more of a concern for women as the current T-shirt style is often cap sleeves.

You could also consider bringing one quick dry hiking blouse/shirt. The collar adds sun protection to your neck, it is loose fitting for the hot weather, and, if it has long sleeves, it keeps the sun off of your arms during the day.

**Number**: Three short sleeve T-Shirts in the warmer time of the year. In the winter on the Camino Frances and on the Northern Route during spring and autumn, two long sleeve and one short sleeve T-shirts.

## Jumpers/Sweaters and Jackets

A light jumper/sweater and/or a fleece jacket that serves as a wind-breaker and is water resistant is ideal and recommended even in summer. Remember it can get chilly in the mountains! Whether you need both of these or only one depends on your time of travel and chosen route. Those who are on the Camino in the midst of winter, or in spring/autumn on the Northern Route will need both. For the Camino in the other 3 seasons one of these will be enough, preferably the jacket as it can be opened when temperatures rise.

## Winter Clothing

Those on the Way during the colder time of the year should remember to take a warm hat/cap and wind-proof gloves. A scarf is normally not necessary, especially if you have a jumper or jacket with a turtle-neck. Some pilgrims swear by wearing a balaclava or a bandana over the face to protect from cold winds. You can also apply fatty face cream generously to further protect you face, especially the lips.

## Multi-use Towel (Pareo/Sarong/Kanga/Kitoy/lava-lava)

Many travellers swear by the microfibre light weight towels. I have to say that I tried them out and I am not impressed by them at all. I prefer a big but lightweight and thin cotton towel. Mine is 1x2 metres, weights less than 100g and was originally meant as a pareo/sarong. I not only use it as a towel, but also as a (head) scarf, additional sun protection, very light (picnic) blanket, skirt, dress, and as an emergency swimming suit. Yes, you can do the latter, if you know how to knot it correctly: simply ask any African friend you have, they will show you how! Alternatively look out for a book entitled "Kangas: 101 Uses, by Jeannette Hanby". It is sometimes still available second-hand at Amazon or other online stores despite being an "oldie, but goldie"! If you buy such a cloth, make sure that the fabric has a high content of cotton (absorption) and is thin (faster drying).

**Number**: One.

**Weight**: 100 gram or less.

## Cap or Hat

A good hat or cap protects from sun and rain, should be fold-able (for storage in the backpack), have a wide brim and a light colour, allow air to circulate, and have a chinstrap to keep it in place when the wind blows strongly. In winter, when the sun is weaker, but the wind stronger and the temperatures lower, a wool cap/toque or balaclava might be better.

**Number**: One is enough.

## What bicigrinos should consider

Pilgrims that bike the Camino, often called jokingly *bicigrinos* (*bici* is short for bike in Spanish), dress themselves in two main fashions. The first one is pretty close to how pilgrims on foot dress and is often preferred by those that bike in a more relaxed way. The second is the more sportive and aerodynamic "proper" cycling gear so to speak; not unlike what you expect to find on the Tour de France and other racing events. The latter ones should note that, while the neighbours on the Camino are pretty much used to seeing pilgrims in all kind of fashions, they will still appreciate it if you turn up in "street clothes" at Church or in restaurants.

## First Aid & Blister Kit

What you pack into your first aid kit depends largely on your own knowledge about first aid plus your known personal weak points health-wise. Remember that Spain has pharmacies, lots of them, where you can buy pretty much everything you need. Plus there is an excellent system of health centres and poly-clinics/consultancies that provide care and treatment. Thus, pack only those things you are likely to need and keep amounts to a minimum. It is better to make your own, personalized kit rather than buying a store-made one, as this way you only carry the things you know you need and know how to use. The simple first aid kit that I use includes the following:

- 1 roll of wide plaster or sport tape
- 1 roll of Micropore (a paper plaster/bandage). Wide is better as you can half them when you need a narrower strip.
- 1 elastic bandage for emergency bandaging of sprained ankles and the like
- 1 small bottle of disinfectant or medical alcohol - small I said!
- 5-10 sterile compresses
- A few painkiller tablets
- All medications that I regularly take
- 2-3 sachets of oral re-hydration mix
- 2 to 3 syringes filled with iodine (see below) either in liquid form or as cream
- A few ready-made wound dressings
- Perhaps a few Compeed®/second skin plasters/bandages (see below)
- A few silicon gel toe caps, if necessary

A word to nurses, doctors and other members of the medical profession that plan to do the pilgrimage: Obviously there is a huge temptation to take a professional first aid kit with you. Fight it! The emergency and rescue system on the Camino is very well organized and equipped. There is no need for you to carry a whole hospital on your back! At the most, I would suggest taking a Guedel Air Kit in the most common sizes and a pocket mask with you. But only if it makes YOU feel better ...

## Blisters

### Prevention and Treatment

Hopefully you will get a few blisters when training at home! No, I am not mean, really not! The problem with blisters is that there is no miracle cure that works equally for everybody, allowing you to continue on the next morning with the least discomfort possible despite the blisters you got the previous day. Remember that you will need to walk on, even if you have a few blisters, to reach Santiago. Some pilgrims swear by Compeed® or other second skin plasters/bandages; others start to swear when they hear the name. More regarding this further below. Here are the most important points to bear in mind when it comes to preventing blisters. Remember, the best blisters are those you don't get!

- Only wear boots/shoes that are well broken in and comfortable.

- Two pairs of socks are better than one, as friction will occur between the socks, not between your skin and the socks/shoes.

- Wash and dry the inner pair of socks daily - the outer pair less often.

- Don't shower in the mornings as this only macerates the skin and makes it more susceptible to blisters.

- For the same reasons, no foot soaks until you have reached the end of your walking day and the *refugio*.

- Never use powder on your feet. When they start to sweat, the powder will clump and rub and cause a skin wound.

- Cream your feet generously at least twice daily with Nivea®, Neutrogena® or the like.

- During rests, if possible, take off shoes and socks and put your feet up (for example on your backpack) to let them rest and to reduce swelling.

- Hot spots and any other areas of discomfort, however light, should be taken care of immediately before a real blister develops.

- In the evenings, wash your feet thoroughly, give them a soak where possible, check for any signs of problems and treat accordingly, and cream generously.

**The better care you take of your feet,
the further they will carry you!**

***Pilgrim Anecdote***

*Especially in summer I have made the following interesting observation in many refugios: Pilgrims that had walked the whole day without a single blister arrived at a stream or fountain and decided to soak their feet in it to cool them down and nearly all of those that did this got blisters during the last kilometres to the refugio. Why? Wet skin means soft and macerated skin that blisters more easily. Therefore keep your feet as dry as possible while walking and wait to have a refreshing foot soak when you have arrived at the refugio. If you can't resist the stream or fountain, dry your feet off well and then let them dry out completely in the sun, at least 15 minutes, to be on the safe side. And don't forget to put foot cream on them again before you tackle those last kilometres.*

\*\*\*

## Compeed®, or no Compeed® ?

Compeed® and similar products from other manufacturers are also called "second skin", and that is what they do best. When you have lost/rubbed off part of your skin through chafing or when a blister bursts of its own accord, a Compeed® will alleviate pain quickly and allow for walking on as it replaces the lost skin. But they have never worked for me in the prevention of blisters or in the treatment of blisters that were still intact. The main disadvantage with Compeed® and the like is that a) if the feet are sweating the Compeed® tends to move and can rip open the blister even further and b) their inner layer, the active ingredient, tends to become liquid when feet are sweaty or the blister oozes a lot of liquid and this very sticky material is close to impossible to wash out of socks. Plus, when it then hardens in the socks, it can rub and produce even more blisters.

For rubbed-off skin or blisters that have lost their skin by accident, Compeed® is a very good product and a pilgrim life saver. But in my opinion, it is not good for preventing blisters or treating blisters that are still closed. In all cases, if you use Compeed®, you should always tape it around its borders to make sure it stays where you put it and to prevent the liquid oozing into your socks.

## Needle and Thread Do NOT belong in Blisters!

*\*\*\*Pilgrim Anecdote\*\*\**

*Attention, not for weak stomachs! They were two Italian pilgrims that limped into the refugio. One hobbled because he was burdened with two backpacks and the other because he could only walk on his heels. As I removed the bandages around the feet of the latter out streamed not only the pus, but also some detached toe nails. A "helpful" person had treated this pilgrim's blisters with the "thread method" and a heavy infection was the result of this. Quickly I bandaged the feet with fresh and clean dressings and took him straight to the doctor at the health centre. This pilgrim had to give up his pilgrimage for that year and spent over a week in hospital where he was treated with intravenous antibiotics. Thankfully, an amputation of one or more of his toes was avoided at the very last minute.*

\*\*\*

**The "thread method" is an outdated blister treatment that should really be retired to a museum.** It consists of putting a sometimes disinfected thread through a blister and leaving it there, the idea being to better drain the blister. This thread not only causes a foreign body irritation, but also acts as a wick through which germs and bacteria can enter the blister and cause an infection. Not all "thread method" situations are as bad as the one described above - but why risk it? Especially if there are safer and better methods available!

## So what is the best blister treatment?

Do you remember that I mentioned above, in the first aid kit list, syringes filled with iodine (either liquid or in cream form)? Here their secret shall be revealed:

**Very Important: NEVER use Iodine or similar on people that have an allergy to it and/or have any thyroid related problems!**

1. Shower first
2. Wash and disinfect your hands.
3. Disinfect the blister and its surroundings well and open it either with a sterile injection needle or with a disinfected pair of sharp nail scissors. What you want to do is make an opening that is large enough to drain the blister but leaves the skin over the blister intact. A small triangular incision of 2-3 mm works best.
4. Be careful: If the blister is under a lot of pressure the liquid contained will splash out with force! Cover the area where you will make the small cut with a sterile compress so that no one gets sprayed with it.
5. Apply some pressure on said compress to empty the blister as much as possible. This hurts a bit as air comes in contact with the raw flesh inside the blister, but this pain will ease quickly.
6. Make a little package out of a sterile compress and bandage/plaster/tape it, applying some pressure, to the healthy skin surrounding the blister. The pressure will prevent the blister from refilling overnight.
7. If you don't have any contraindications to using iodine (known as Betadine in Spain and readily available in every single Spanish pharmacy) you can fill the blister

with it. Use either one of your pre-filled syringes or fill one now, with iodine, and insert the iodine in to the blister. **Attention!** If you use liquid iodine it will burn like hell for a few minutes, if you use iodine cream it will burn a bit less, but still hurt a lot!

8. If you are afraid of needles you can still use just the syringe, without the needle, and enter its opening carefully in to the blister and apply the iodine like that. Make sure, by massaging a bit, that the iodine enters in all corners and folds of the blister. The iodine cream especially needs a bit of encouraging.

9. Now cover, as above, with a package made from a sterile compress and cover with a plaster/bandage, taking care that it only sticks to healthy skin and not to the skin on the blister itself.

10. The idea here is that, with a bit of pressure, the skin above the blister once again attaches itself to the flesh below.

11. If walking is still painful the next morning, here is a trick to try and relieve some pressure on the blister. Buy a Spontex® kitchen cloth, the blue ones are normally the thickest, that are made from cellulose and can be found in every Spanish grocery shop (*tienda*). Cut it to size, leaving a hole where your blister is and tape it to your skin, again attaching it on healthy, blister free skin. This provides easy pressure relief!

12. You should never cut off the skin that covers your blister until new, strong, and resistant skin has formed. Also remember to keep the dressings clean, change them after every shower and, when a dressing is no longer required, cream the old skin over the blister well to keep it soft and elastic. Otherwise it will dry out, become hard, and cause another blister!

### And if the blister refills again?

I will repeat here what I have told countless pilgrims: "Open the blister again, empty it and re-bandage/re-plaster applying pressure until the blister gets tired of bothering you or the two of you arrive together in Santiago!"

**Three important things to end the theme of blisters:**

- Unless you are a medical professional and know what you are doing, only treat your own blisters and let other pilgrims treat theirs!

- Always watch out for signs of infections (heat, swelling, pus and/or pain) and go to a health centre, or at least to a pharmacy, at the slightest sign of an infection.

- Those who tend to get blisters under their toe nails should bring silicon toe caps from home as they can be difficult to find on the Camino.

## Medication and Prescriptions

If you suffer from a chronic illness, frequently have a re-occurring health issue (allergy, hay fever, headaches etc.) or are on regular medication, you should first discuss your plans to make the pilgrimage with your doctor and then get enough medication to cover the whole stay away from home. Additionally, it is wise to bring an international, private prescription in case you lose your medication or similar. Tell your doctor to note on said prescription not only the brand name but also the generic name of the active ingredient(s), as not all brands are available in Spain but most ingredients are. If you are on a very rare form of medication, you should ask beforehand if it will be available in Spain. A good place to start asking these questions is this official website: http://mapausa.org/eng/food.htm

If you suffer from hay fever or are generally prone to allergies, don't forget to take your favourite antihistamine. If you suffer frequently from headaches, bring a few pain killers. An upset tummy or diarrhoea can happen easily and a few sachets with re-hydration powder will help you to re-balance the electrolytes and water in your body back to normal. In short, bring enough to get you over one problem, until you feel up to going to a pharmacy for re-stocking, but don't bring your whole medication cabinet!

All medication should be packaged safely and include their fact sheet. Old film containers are useful for carrying small amounts of medications.

If you are on some sort of medication that isn't allowed/available in Spain, you will need to bring a translated prescription and a covering letter from your doctor. See the website mentioned above. The truth is that controls are pretty lax, but why run the risk of getting your medication confiscated?

It is beyond the scope of this book to cover all possible scenarios, but a chronic illness or disability doesn't mean you have to give up your dream of a pilgrimage to Santiago de Compostela. If you suffer from chronic illnesses like those that, for example, affect the proper function of the heart, kidney, or lungs or you have diabetes, you should always consult your doctor before embarking on the Camino.

Chronic illness is not an absolute obstacle to becoming a pilgrim, but requires good planning, preparation, training, and perhaps even a companion. It is not unusual for diabetics to finish the Camino successfully and dozens of wheelchair users achieve the same every year.

## More Useful Things

### Rubbish Bag

No, not as an emergency rain cover (though it does work as that also!) but as an extra way of protecting your gear. You don't need to splash out on a professional waterproof inner liner for your backpack. Simply line your backpack with a big rubbish bag that is made out of strong material and it will protect all that is packed inside from water damage.

Those who walk in a rainy season should also get an additional, smaller one, for their sleeping bag. There is nothing more annoying than to unpack your backpack after a hard and rainy walking day only to discover that your sleeping bag got wet.

**Number**: One big one (a few litres bigger than your backpack) plus a smaller one for your sleeping bag.

### Pocket Knife

All you need is a simple pocket knife with a cork screw for *vino* aficionados, or a bottle opener for beer lovers, and with a can opener and a small pair of scissors for everyone. Thus equipped you will be able to cut bread, cheese, and sausage for your roadside picnic and open a nice bottle of Rioja wine in the evening. A small pair of scissors is practical for cutting bandages/plasters and wound dressings. If you already plan to carry nail scissors in your first aid kit you will NOT need another one on your pocket knife. Tweezers are also handy if they are included in your pocket knife, but things like a magnifying glass or a saw are less so.

What is the worst case scenario if your pocket knife doesn't have a specific tool or function? Most of the time the answer will be, nothing serious. If you think that you will only eat in restaurants and bars and you will never have a wayside picnic or cook in a *refugio* then you don't need one at all!

**Extra Tip**: Depending on when you have last used it, it might be a good idea to give your pocket knife a good clean, oil it and, most importantly, sharpen the blade.

## Safety Pins

Better than clothes pegs! Safety pins can be used to hang clothes for drying on a clothes line, fix bandages, and even to replace a lost button.

**Extra Tip**: If your freshly washed clothes are still a bit damp the next morning and it is dry and sunny, you can fix them to the back of your backpack to dry while  you are walking. Safety pins are better for this than clothes pegs as they are safer (sorry for the bad pun).

# What some pilgrims might need

Before you pack anything from this list honestly ask yourself : What would be the worst case scenario if I did NOT take xyz with me?

## Sleeping Pad

I know a lot of pilgrims that don't take one with them but they do have their uses.

If you are walking in the main season on the Camino Francés you should know that sometimes there are simply not enough beds for all pilgrims and the *refugios* can then only offer you a bit of extra floor to sleep on. If that happens, or if you decide to sleep in the porch of the nearest church or somewhere else outside, you will appreciate even a few millimetres of foam between your hip bones and the floor. During the day you can sit on a sleeping pad or stretch out on it and have a nice *siesta* in the shade.

If you take one or not depends mostly on your own wish for comfort. But if, on the other hand, you know that you will always stay in pre-booked hotels and hostels, you will not need one. When I say sleeping pad I mean the normal foam ones, not the self inflatable ones like Thermarest® brand which are far too heavy.

If you want to save a few more grams while on the Way in the low season or on a less frequented Camino, and thus can be sure to nearly always have a bed in the *refugios*, you could consider taking a smaller, lighter foam mat that is reflective (aluminium). They are a good compromise between weight and comfort, but better for *siestas* and the like rather than for a whole night's sleep.

**Extra Tip**: Consider cutting the sleeping mat down to get rid of weight and volume. For a minimal length suggestion, ensure that your shoulders and hips will be on the mat if you have to sleep on it.

**Number**: One.

**Weight**: Between 150 and 250g, depending on the model.

## Ear Plugs

Traditionally, you will sleep in the dormitories of the pilgrim *refugios* and thus you can count it as a true miracle of the Way if you have a night when none of your fellow pilgrims snore! Ear plugs not only keep the snoring out, they can also be useful if the village you stay in has a *Fiesta* and the music and dance take place in close proximity to the refuge and go on until the wee hours.

**Shopping Tip**: Try to find ear plugs that are made out of soft foam which doesn't have to be kneaded soft. They tend to be more comfortable then the wax ones.

**Number**: Bring a pair or two and buy new ones when the need arises as they are widely available in Spanish pharmacies and, btw, called *"tapones para los oídos"*.


## Bed bugs Prevention

In places where many people share a sleeping space, bed bugs also feel at home. It was like this in the medieval ages and unfortunately over the last few years the bed bugs have made their "comeback" to the Camino de Santiago. They are called *chinches* in Spanish and as with blisters, prevention is the best cure! Bed bugs can happen in the best and cleanest houses, even pilgrims who have slept in luxury hotels have been bitten by them and simple traditional *refugios* can be completely bedbug free.

What can you do to prevent befriending bed bugs on the way and prevent taking this completely unwanted souvenir home with you?

First of all, essential oils such as lavender, tea tree or neem oil do **NOT** help! A bed bug isn't the slightest bit interested in how you smell: they orientate themselves via your body warmth and especially via the $CO_2$ that you exhale. This helps them to find their personal blood donor and food resource - you! Silk sleeping bag inserts or mite-proof sleeping bag covers don't help a lot. You still can be bitten on the hands, arms, neck and face. And they will still crawl into your backpack, given the slightest chance, wanting to come home with you!

The only products that have shown some degree of effectiveness are Permethrin® impregnated sheets (under the sleeping bag) or Permethrin® impregnated sleeping bag covers. But the bed bugs may already be resistant to Permethrin®. Another possibility is to soak all your equipment (back pack, sleeping bag and perhaps even your clothes) with a product that contains Permethrin® and DEET (see appendix for some product suppliers) and thus impregnate your gear yourself. Just keep in mind that these chemicals can have negative side-effects on humans and read the instructions that come with the products very carefully!

Other tips for preventing bed bugs are:

- Try to stay up to date on the situation and frequently ask *hospitaleros*, and those few pilgrims that are walking the Way back(wards), what they know about bed bugs in the next few *refugios*. This informal system of information exchange is nicknamed "Radio Camino" by the way - listen to it!

- Never put your backpack on or under a bed and avoid leaning it against a wall.

- The upper bunk bed, where that applies, seems to be a tiny bit safer.

- Try to avoid becoming a "bed bug taxi" and transporting them further along the Way or even worse, taking them home with you.

- Heat kills all life stages of the bed bug reliably, so wash and dry what can be washed and dried at the highest temperature possible as often as possible and certainly at the slightest suspicion that you have "caught the bug".

- Put what can't be washed in the full sun; just be careful not to fry your electronics.

- Very low temperatures (below -18C for 72h) also kill all life stages of bed bugs, but a freezer might be hard to find on the Camino! And who wants to stay for 3 days in the same place? This may be a good method for when you have reached Santiago and have some days there before travelling home.

For bed bug bites, and the frequent allergic reaction that often follows them, anti-histamine creams help. Calamin® lotion is also useful and it is available in Spanish pharmacies. If the itch and the allergic reaction are heavy, anti-histamine tablets might be helpful and if that doesn't help a visit to the local *Centro de Salud* (poly-clinic/health centre) for some anti-histamine or cortisone injections is in order.

For more information about bed bugs and how to prevent getting them, have a look at this website:

http://bedbugger.com/

At the moment there are two articles on it that refer to the situation on the Camino:

http://bedbugger.com/2009/09/12/bed-bug-luau-on-the-camino-to-santiago/

http://bedbugger.com/2008/09/12/bed-bugs-on-the-camino-de-santiago-de-compostela/

Despite the fact that they are not very recent, the tips in these articles and on the whole website are still worth reading!

## Sun Protection

### Sun screen

I have seen pilgrims getting sunburnt in November, so you have been warned! Take a good sun cream/blocker with you that has at least a factor of 20SPF or even higher if you are fair skinned. And yes, bring a small bottle/tube directly from home to apply before the first rays of the strong Spanish sun hit you. Even if the Camino is not on the Costa del Sol, the sun can "bite" here and not only in summer.

**Amount**: A small bottle for the first few days; more can be always be bought later on the Camino.

### Sun Glasses

These depend on how light sensitive your eyes are. If you are like me when I was younger and can stand bright sun shine without a problem, you will not need them. If, on the other hand, you are like me when I got older and suffer from light sensitive eyes, you will need a pair on the Camino.

People who wear glasses anyway should consider those that adjust from light to dark with the amount of UV light. You can get them with dioptre adjustment. This type is also known as photo-chromic or photo-chromatic glasses which are very handy when walking into a dark bar from the bright sunlight or vice versa.

## Glasses or Contact Lenses?

Even dedicated contact lens wearers should seriously consider leaving them at home and going on the Camino bespectacled. Why? The Way can be very dusty when dry and you know what that does to eyes that have contact lenses in them. The essentials for taking care of your lenses also adds weight. And last, but not least, you have to take a pair of emergency glasses in most cases anyway. Those who can't or won't live without contacts, should consider switching to daily disposables to save on the weight of the care products.

**Number**: Glasses, prescription for glasses, and if necessary replacement glasses (depending on your eyesight without them) OR contact lenses and care products for them, if not using daily disposables, and replacement glasses and prescription.

## Stick, Sticks or no Sticks?

Modern pilgrims often walk with one or two telescopic sticks which resemble ski poles and are about waist high. I have done all three so far, walking with one, two or no sticks at all. Every method has its advantages and disadvantages. Those who are used to walking with sticks should obviously take them. Those who have never walked with sticks should try it out at home first as it takes a bit of getting used to. The traditional pilgrim's staff, which you still see in use on the Camino, is made from wood, often beautifully carved and typically taller than its owner.

The main disadvantage of sticks is that you forget them easily and it is no fun to walk a few kilometres back and forth just to retrieve them. That happens more often than you think; ask any experienced pilgrim or *hospitalero*! Also transporting them on aeroplanes can prove to be problematic, especially with the full sized ones. The telescopic ones will fit in to your check-in luggage but the longer ones have to be checked in separately as an oversize item.

The main advantage of using sticks shows itself when walking downhill as they tend, when used correctly, to take the weight off the knees. If the terrain becomes a bit difficult, they also help you to keep your balance.

Those who tend to have problems with their knees should consider walking with two modern, telescopic sticks. Those who only need a stick when the terrain becomes a bit difficult will only need one; perhaps a traditional one? Then it is a beautiful idea to bring said stick from home and to decorate it yourself with carvings. Such a staff can be taken to your pilgrim's blessing at home and will then become a very special support for you on the Camino.

**From my own experience**: I prefer walking with only one stick and one that doubles, if I take my camera with me, as a mono-pod.

### (Emergency) Food

Did I mention already that there are shops in Spain? I thought I did! Seriously, there is no reason whatsoever to bring food to Spain. *Frutos secos* (dried fruits and nuts) are available in every shop and in bigger towns you will find whole shops dedicated to selling only dried fruits, nuts and chocolate. As a snack on the way bread, cheese, olives, and sausages are readily available and easy to transport.

### Sewing Kit

Please don't take your whole sewing box; you will not need it. A simple sewing kit like that which you find in hotel rooms is sufficient. A sturdy needle and thread are more important than having the right coloured thread. Note that those who carry safety pins and duct tape can do most emergency repairs on the way and then can ask in the next *refugio* for needle and thread.

## Duct tape

A rip in your rain poncho or shoe? A torn off buckle on your backpack? The battery compartment of your camera refuses to close properly? No more plaster tape but the dressing on your blister slides around and rubs? Enter duct tape, a really useful first aid piece for your equipment and for you. A small roll, or even half a role, weighs only a little but can help a lot in an emergency and will keep you afloat until the problematic piece of clothing or equipment can be taken care of by the hands of a professional in the next town.

## Clothes Line

A piece of clothes line, (some pilgrims swear by the "stretchy variety") can be handy, but normally clothes lines are provided in the *refugios*. If the clothes line also fulfils other purposes (emergency rain poncho belt), take it with you. If not, better to leave it at home. Please take care when putting up a clothes line in a dormitory or elsewhere so that it doesn't obstruct the passageways, especially at night!

### ***Pilgrim Anecdote***

*The hospitalera is always the last to go to bed and the first one to get up. But admittedly I wouldn't have imagined in my wildest nightmares that this could be so dangerous. To get to my own room I had to tip-toe through the pilgrim's dormitory in the dark night. One evening I nearly strangled myself on a clothes line that a pilgrim had very inconveniently put up at neck height across my door.*

\*\*\*

# Luxury Items

## Cell phone

I have walked the Camino with and without a cell phone. Again, both have advantages and disadvantages and it is up to you to make a decision.

**With**: In an emergency, help can be called quickly (remember the international emergency number **112**). If you have concerned family members, relatives/parents or friends at home, you might want to be reachable by text or phone call.

**Without**: Going without a cell phone is a unique way to remain undisturbed and to be able to concentrate on the here and now and the essentials of life. For the rest of the discussion, please read again the chapter "Technology and a thousand year old pilgrimage route" at the beginning of this book.

## Camera

Photos are one of the most cherished souvenirs from the Camino and keep memories alive for years. Before you pack your complete camera gear take a moment to consider how you want to use these photos in the future. If you only want to take snapshots to show them to family and friends at home and to share them on Facebook and other social media platforms, or on your own website or blog, the built-in camera on your cell phone can be completely sufficient. If you have greater expectations on image quality you should consider packing a good digital compact (the Canon G series is certainly worth a look). If you are only satisfied by really professional image quality, then pack the (D)SLR, but please, only with one lens.

**Extra Tip**: As a photographer I take my own DSLR with me on the Camino and as a lens I pack a 18-55 mm zoom. As my main photographic subjects are landscapes, other pilgrims, architecture, plants and animals, this is completely sufficient for me. Alternatively, providing less range and requiring more "zooming with the feet" but giving even better image quality whilst carrying less weight, a fixed 50 mm lens is also a good choice.

**Extra Tips:** Don't forget enough memory card(s) and a (universal) charger for all your gear.

Obviously I don't carry a heavy tripod but instead I have a mono-pod that I also use as a walking stick - killing two birds with one stone. An alternative to this would be to take a small "gorilla pod" with you that can be attached to a variety of surfaces.

## Netbook / Tablet / iPad (mini)

If you plan to write so much that it would be uncomfortable on a cell phone / smart phone or you need a computer for other purposes, like writing a Camino guide, you should consider taking a net book, iPad (mini) or the like. Internet cafés can be found in many places along the way and offer the burning of videos and photos on CDs for a reasonable rate. Apart from this, you need to keep in mind that a notebook or similar is yet another piece of gear to worry about (weather/theft) and that needs to be charged regularly. If you don't need it for professional reasons it is best to leave it at home.

**Extra Tips:** If you take a smart phone and want to type your diary more comfortably on it you might consider taking a very small and light-weight USB keyboard with you.

If you are technically minded you can use a service like Sugarsync (https://www.sugarsync.com) to back up your data (photos!) into the internet cloud whenever you are in a wifi-hotspot – which are now quite frequent on the Camino.

## Diary, Pen, Scrapbook, Drawing materials

Those who have decided to use the Camino as a sort of technology detox should write important addresses and phone numbers on the last few pages of a normal paper notebook which could also be used as a diary. Many pilgrims, even if they don't feel this temptation at home, develop the urge on the Camino to jot down their thoughts, feelings, and experiences on paper. A normal paper notebook and pen are completely sufficient for this. When the notebook is full and the pen empty, they both can be easily replaced in one of the many shops on the way.

Those who are unhappy when not being able to draw or to paint or those who want to keep a scrapbook style diary should take drawing materials. Just remember that every coloured pen contributes its own weight!

## Torch / Flashlight / Headlight

Here you also have two very different opinions among pilgrims. Some wouldn't go without some form of flashlight. Others, like me, can do without. What do pilgrims use a flashlight for?

- To find the toilet at night - For this, if one's night-sight is bad, you can also use the light of your cell phone display (If you are taking one!)

- To read in the dark/at night - Common rooms in the *refugios* are normally open at night and can be used for this but even the biggest bookworm (somebody like me) is usually far too tired in the evenings from the efforts of the day to be able to read a lot at night.

- To find the way early in the morning - This is a difficult one. Starting early in the morning to avoid the greatest heat of the day is one thing. To start in the dark just to race to the next *refugio* to secure a bed is another. Please consider why you are doing the pilgrimage. Is it only to have a bed at night? You, hopefully, have a bed at home and thus there is no reason to dedicate a whole pilgrimage to this goal! Those who start in the dark with a flashlight have a few other disadvantages. Many pilgrims simply loose the Way in the dark as their eyes don't adapt properly as they are continuously blinded by the light of other pilgrim's flashlights - or their own. And that has periodically led to sprained ankles and broken ribs as you can't see the uneven ground on the Way. Also it is much more difficult to see the (sometimes faded) yellow arrows (route marker) in the dark. Apart from this, you also miss seeing everything that there is to see on the first few kilometres of each day.

- Even in summer, when sunrise is early, there are still 4 to 5 hours of reasonable walking temperature at the beginning of the day before it gets really hot. That is enough to cover a distance of 20 to 25 kilometres. If you want to walk more, but don't want to rush, you can have a *siesta* in the shade during the strongest heat and can then walk a few more kilometres late in the afternoon/early evening.

To take a torch or not? Those who still believe they need one should consider taking a hands free torch (head lamp) that has the ability to dim the strength of the beam. Please don't put it on in the dormitory and flash it at your poor fellow pilgrims that really wanted to sleep a bit longer!

## Songbook and /or small Musical Instruments

Those who love to sing or to make music could pack a small, lightweight songbook with his favourite tunes or even make your own songbook. A light musical instrument, like a flute or a harmonica, can bring joy to you and your fellow pilgrims (If you play it well!) Avoid taking anything particularly heavy, fragile, or valuable on the Camino unless you are, as happened a few years ago, a professional music ensemble doing the Camino in medieval costumes and with the respective instruments, to collect money for a good cause.

# Symbols

## Scallop Shell

For over a thousand years, the scallop shell has been the traditional sign of the pilgrimage to Santiago de Compostela. The actual tradition is to bring a shell back from Santiago and not to carry it to Santiago as the scallop shell served, in the past, as one of the proofs that the pilgrim had actually "made it". That has changed in modern times and nowadays nearly every pilgrim carries a scallop shell around their neck or on their backpack from the very beginning of their Camino. Scallop shells, with or without a St. James cross painted on them, can be obtained at home via your local St. James association, bought on Amazon, or by asking your local fishmonger/fish restaurant for one. They are also available along the Camino in some *albergues* and shops. Pilgrims prefer often that half of the shell that is more concave than flat, but both are perfectly acceptable. In the old times the pilgrim shell also served as a way of drinking out of shallow puddles or streams and are still used by many Churches as a baptism shell.

Many of the legends that surround the Camino and the person of St. James feature the shell prominently. The most well known one is that of a young knight being thrown off his horse into the sea and miraculously rescued by St. James. As the knight emerged from the water, legend has it, he was completely covered in scallop shells. Another, less known one, describes the fate of a pilgrim that ran out of water while crossing the Alto del Perdón near Pamplona. He was then tempted by the devil that promised him water if he worshipped him. The pious pilgrim refused and the devil disappeared and shortly after the pilgrim met St. James, disguised as a pilgrim, who gave him fresh water to drink from his own scallop shell.

Therefore you will usually find every statue of St. James adorned with at least one scallop shell, as long as he is depicted as Santiago Peregrino, St. James the pilgrim. If he is depicted as Santiago Matamoros, St. James the Moor-Slayer, this is rarely the case. There are many more legends and theories that connect St. James, the Camino, and the scallop shell but that is material for another book.

**Extra Tip**: If you need or want to drill your own hole into the shell, do so slowly and by hand, as they are brittle and break easily. Don't apply too much pressure and take your time. You can then thread a leather or other cord through the hole and carry it around your neck or on your backpack.

## Stone

Another pilgrim tradition is to leave a stone that you have brought from home at the Cruz de Ferro (Iron Cross) in the mountains of Léon. At 1500 metres above sea level, it is one of the highest points on the Camino Francés. This stone symbolizes the laying down of your own worries, fears, concerns and in general all that you want to leave behind. By the way, the tradition speaks of leaving only a stone; there is already enough litter cluttering up the cross!

The historical origin of the Iron Cross is hidden in the mists of time, but various theories about it exist. The most widely accepted one is that it developed out of the Celtic and Roman tradition of marking important crossroads and passes with a mound of stones. Later, as Christianity took over, a tall wooden pillar with a small iron cross, hence the name, was erected and the tradition of leaving a stone as a symbol for ones "burdens" developed.

**Extra Tip**: The stone doesn't need to be huge nor heavy; it is a symbol!

## What a Pilgrim, in Most Cases, Doesn't Need

The following things are not necessary for those that plan to make their pilgrimage on one of the Spanish or French main routes as these routes are well marked and have an excellent infrastructure. If you walk other Ways, or have an animal companion, things might be different for you.

### Tent

A tent is only needed by those that walk beyond the official pilgrim's routes and/or have an animal companion with them. If you plan to walk one of the main Ways in France and/or Spain you don't need a tent! In the case of a long distance pilgrim it might be a good idea to use the tent as long as you need it and to send it home as soon as you are about to join the Camino Francés (for addresses of some French and Spanish post offices, see appendix).

In all cases, the tent should be as light as possible. A bivouac style tent is enough for one person and shouldn't weigh more than 1500g. I used one like this on my pilgrimage from Santiago to Rome and was very happy with it. As I am not too tall, I simply put my backpack at the foot end and the remaining space was still comfortable enough for me to sleep in.

If you are two or more persons, you can divide the different tent components between you, that way the extra weight per pilgrim is not too much.

Don't forget that a tent should only be packed up if it has completely dried, which can take some time depending on the amount of morning dew it has collected.

Remember that if you are already doubting that you will need a tent, chances are good that you don't need one! And anyway, wild camping is prohibited in Spain and not every pilgrim *refugio* will have a meadow where they will allow you to pitch your tent.

## Maps

A good Camino guide will have all the necessary maps you will need and in France, and especially in Spain, the system of way marking (yellow arrows/shell symbols) is so good that you will rarely refer to the maps in your guide. As with other "might be useful" things, if you are only on the Way in Spain and France and stick to the main pilgrim routes, you don't need to carry extra detailed maps. They are heavy! Those who start from further afield and therefore cross regions which are rarely or not at all way marked, will need maps. The best way to reduce the amount of maps you carry is to either take them with you in electronic form or to regularly send back home those that you don't need anymore. Or you can get somebody at home to send them ahead for you, so that you can pick them up at a post office (*correos*) while on your way. Some useful addresses for this are in the appendix plus some sources for maps.

## GPS

Since the GPS has been invented, or at least became affordable for the average person, you will meet pilgrims with one on the Camino.

### ***Pilgrim Anecdote***

*The first time I saw a GPS, it was in the hand of an American pilgrim. I was helping review her backpack contents and decide what to send, for weight reduction reasons, ahead to Santiago. The funny thing was that it was a gift from her overly concerned children who were afraid that Mommy would get lost in Spain but she couldn't use it as she had forgotten the manual back at home in the USA. I think it is needless to say that we put the GPS on the ever-growing pile of things to be sent off to Santiago.*

\*\*\*

A GPS on the main routes in Spain and France is, in my opinion, as necessary as an extra blister on the foot of a pilgrim. **Exception**: Those who walk off the beaten track and/or want to record their Camino for further use in a guide could consider carrying one. Just make yourself very familiar with it as they are not as easy to use as their advertising tells you, especially if you want to use it for recording your position and progress.

## Vitamins, Minerals & Food Supplements

Some pilgrim's backpacks give the impression that they have emptied out not one, but several health stores! Don't forget that the Spanish cuisine is one of the healthiest in the world and if you simply follow the local diet, you can save a lot of money and weight while living as healthy, or even healthier, than you do at home. Bananas and dried fruits and nuts replace mineral tablets and prevent muscle cramps, while fresh fruit and vegetables replace vitamins in tablet form.

## Stove & Cooking Gear

It is true that some *refugios* don't have a kitchen and some *refugio* kitchens have little to no cooking gear, especially those in Galicia. But is it worth it, because of this, to carry a camping stove in your backpack? If there is no kitchen nor microwave in the *refugio,* you will survive your start in the morning without having a cup of tea or mug of coffee, believe me! The added weight of stove and cooking gear will burden your backpack so much that I seriously doubt their occasional use will make up for this. Pretty much every village on the way will have a café or bar where you can have a coffee, tea, hot chocolate, and something to eat.

**Exception**:   Those who come from further afield and are camping will appreciate the option of cooking to save some money on a longer pilgrimage. When you arrive at the Spanish border this gear can be sent home, or ahead to Santiago, as you have now arrived in "pilgrim civilization".

## Hair Dryer, Electric Toothbrush, and other fancy items

Here a few more things that pilgrims have taken on the Way and barely ever used. This list is compiled from my own experience and that of dozens of other *hospitaleros* and pilgrims:

Electric toothbrush, hair dryer, manicure set, beard trimmer, electric nose hair remover, hammock, mosquito net, Packsafe® lock and, drum roll please – a surgical mask (The pilgrim ignored my question as to why it was in his backpack).

# Packing and Carrying

By now you should have your main gear together and have compiled your personal packing list with the customizable documents which you can find in the link below. We now come to the final selection and the best way of packing and testing your gear. You need to do this well ahead, before the planned start of your Camino, for training and fine tuning purposes.

## Creating your personal packing list

1. Download my packing list template from this link: http://www.caminosantiago.eu/packing-list

   either in PDF or DOC format, whatever you prefer.

2. Edit the packing list by first removing all items you will not need, for example winter gloves when you are walking in the summer.

3. Read, again, the chapter concerning each item of equipment and decide which version/number YOU want to take. For example, one tall walking stick or two telescopic ones.

4. Print packing list and proceed.

## Fine tuning your gear

Put all that you plan to take on your bed or on the floor and, once again, (I do know that I repeat this tip quite frequently) place every single item in your hand and ask yourself the following questions:

- Can I replace this item with another one that has a multi purpose use?
- Is there anything on this item that I can remove without negatively affecting its function?
- What is the worst case scenario if I don't take this item with me?
- Can I get this item in a smaller or simpler version that weighs less?

Remember, now is your best and easiest chance to save weight. I am sure you will be thankful for each gram less in your backpack once you are walking the Camino. Now weigh every single item in your pile and note down its weight on your packing list - this way you can more effectively pick out the worst offenders. Be sure to also list the weight of those items you are not completely sure about and add up this total. Most of the time pilgrims don't realize how several "perhaps nice to have" items that each don't weigh much, do add up to a considerable amount when totalled together.

## Correct packing and carrying of a backpack

Packing a backpack is an art that is learned with experience. Here are a few tips:

The items you will need during the day (Camino guide, water, snacks, first aid kit and the like) should be easily reachable in your backpack and/or its outer pockets, in your trouser pockets, or in your belt pouch.

If rain is a possibility, then your rain gear should be easily accessible.

Temperature sensitive things such as food in warm weather or appliances that rely on battery power in cold weather, should be buried deep in the backpack to protect them from the heat or cold.

Things that go/work together should be in the same container or bag. For your picnic/wayside snack you can either use a Tupperware®/plastic container or even a zip lock bag. Dirty clothes belong in one plastic bag, body care products in a leak-safe zip lock bag, clean clothes in a clean plastic bag, and so on.

Sleeping bag, sandals/shoes for the *refugio* and everything that you only need in the evening, after the day's walk, can be buried in the depth of your pack.

Copies of your documents belong in a plastic cover and should be buried deep in your backpack, ideally close to really smelly socks!

## Weight Distribution

A correctly packed backpack carries itself - nearly. A badly packed one interferes negatively with your body balance and can quickly cause pain in the back, knees, and shoulders. It is important that the backpack is adjusted to the height of the pilgrim, (many packs have this option), and that the hip belt and shoulder straps are adjusted so that the main weight of the backpack rests on the hips and not on the shoulders.

More tips:

Heavy things should be packed/carried as close to your back (point of gravity) as possible to avoid the backpack pushing you forward or pulling you backward or to one side.

Try to avoid attaching anything to the outside of your bag, especially when it is windy. Exception: Clothes you want to dry. Here is my own packing system to get you started:

- Sleeping bag and sandals for the *refugio* end up in the lower compartment of my backpack, protected by a rubbish bag.
- The sleeping pad, if I take one, is fold-able, not a roll, and goes directly in the front of the lower compartment, this way I have it handy if I feel like taking a *siesta* or a break and don't want to sit on cold or wet ground.
- I line the main compartment with a large garbage bag and into this goes pretty much all the rest of my belongings.
- Books, and anything else made out of paper or anything else that is heavy, go directly against my back and are protected by a plastic layer (zip lock bag).
- Things that I only need in the *refugio* like clean clothes and my body care kit go in the bottom of the main compartment.
- The remaining space is then filled with the rest of my belongings. The more likely that I may need it that day while walking, like the first aid kit or a change of socks, the higher up they go.

- Things like the Camino guide, snack food, cell phone, and water either go into one of the outside pockets, the pocket in the lid of the backpack or in my belt pouch where I also put all my valuables and papers.

**Extra Tip**: If it is raining, a zip-lock bag helps to protect the Camino guide and still allows for checking how far it is to the next *refugio*.

## *Bicigrinos* and their luggage

Apart from their own belongings, cycling pilgrims also need to carry everything for maintaining and repairing their bikes, either in their bike panniers or, if they are pilgrims with an accompanying vehicle, in that. Check ahead of time to ensure that replacement parts like wheels, tires, and spokes are available for your particular bike model in Spain; especially if you have a model that is not widely used there. It would be a good idea to contact your bike's manufacturer before you start and ask for retail addresses in Spain and/or France that carry the correct replacement parts for your bike model. When pilgrims on bikes do have an accompanying vehicle with them, it is best to bring all that you might need for repair and maintenance from home. This can save time and stress as you don't need to hunt for the right replacement parts in Spain.

Packing your pannier bags follows similar principles to packing a backpack. Put heavy things close to your bike's point of gravity, things you need that day in easy reach, etc. Keep in mind the weight limits of your bike's frame and of your panniers and keep things balanced. This means the weight should be evenly distributed and in such a way that it doesn't push/pull your bike to one side.

If you carry an additional bag on your back, make sure it is a light one and not heavily loaded otherwise it will make it difficult to keep your balance in difficult terrain. Things that can go in a backpack are food for the day and rain gear if rain seems to be a possibility.

**Hint:** In Galicia, rain is always a possibility!

# Pilgrim Chariots and other alternatives

***Pilgrim Anecdote***

*I will never forget the expression on the face of my dear hospitalero colleague as two Brazilian pilgrims walked into the refugio pulling suitcases on wheels behind them! We quickly discovered that this middle-aged couple had read the infamously famous book by Paulo Cuelho and got animated to walk the Camino themselves. Unfortunately they hadn't invested any time in further research about the practical aspects of this pilgrimage. Fortunately they were not poor and could afford to buy themselves a complete outfit of new pilgrim gear, including two backpacks! Two days later, when all was bought and explained to them, they set off into the sunrise and made it safe and sound to Santiago. We know this because they had to return to the refugio to pick up their suitcases and other belongings that we had kept in storage for them.*

\*\*\*

Suitcases on wheels are really not suitable for the Camino, but you may occasionally see backpacks on wheels, in some form or another. Handcarts or chariots that the pilgrim pushes or pulls are the way some pilgrims try to make their burden more manageable. Those who don't want to or can't carry a fully loaded backpack should keep in mind that many parts of the Camino are not really feasible for such carts and that means that you will have to walk along the road instead or put your backpack on your back for those stretches. Pilgrims that have used such carts, and with whom I have spoken, can be roughly divided into two groups: those that loved them, and those that hated them and wished they had brought a normal backpack instead. If you are interested in the different types of pilgrim carts you will find some useful websites in the appendix.

Bicycle trailers are a favourite among those *bicigrinos* that either come from further afield, started from home, or are on the Camino with their children, as these trailers allow you to take more luggage.

## Horse or donkey with carriage, vintage farm tractors, camels, and all else

Yes, even camels have been sighted on the Camino, but rarely. A horse or donkey before a carriage is a slightly more frequent sight and even the odd person has tried to do the pilgrimage on his vintage farm tractor. There's nothing that hasn't been on the Camino. Those who contemplate doing the pilgrimage with one of these more unusual methods of transport will not have it easy exactly, but can be sure to attract a lot of attention!

## *¡Buen Camino!* And a Request

*¡Buen Camino!* is the traditional greeting for pilgrims on the Camino. "Have a good Way!" is not only what the Spaniards wish the pilgrims, it is also how pilgrims greet one another. With a heartfelt *¡Buen Camino!* I now say goodbye to you and I also wish you "*Ultreia y Suseia*", onward and higher, which is the thousand year old greeting of encouragement used by pilgrims in the middle ages when Latin was the language on the Camino.

**If this book was useful to you, would you please take a moment and write a review about it on Amazon?**

And if you have any complaints or suggestions for improvement you can reach me via my Camino website http://www.caminosantiago.eu/kontakt/. I know that the website is mainly in German, my native language, but I do promise you to answer back in English ;-)

# After the Way

For many the most difficult stage of the Camino is the travel back and the arrival home. Here are a few tips that might make this easier for you.

As most pilgrims will not have the time, money, or suitable location to start at their own doorstep to Santiago and then walk back home, it can be a good compromise to plan your return travel in such a way that you walk the last few kilometres home. Perhaps you could even make it a few days or perhaps from the airport to your home? This allows body and soul to re-adjust to "normal life" and modern amenities and hopefully reduces the cultural shock a bit. This is especially important if you have been on the road for many weeks or even months. Another good way to keep the Camino Spirit alive is to join one of the many St. James associations where you can meet other pilgrims.

**Extra Tip:** If you know that you have already been infected with the "Camino bug", and plan to make more pilgrimages in future, it is a good idea to make a note of everything you unpack from your backpack and, for each item, note how often you used it or not. If you compare that second list with your original packing list, which you have hopefully kept, you can see:

- What is still in your backpack - because you needed it.
- What is no longer in your backpack - because you didn't need it and got rid of it.

This will then be the base for your packing list for your next pilgrimage. And with the help of many such packing lists of mine I have written this book!

## Thank Yous

The first and biggest "Thank You" obviously goes to all the pilgrims and *hospitaleros* I have met over the years on the Camino. Without you, this book would not have been written!

A double "Thank You" to my Canadian friend, Daphne Hnatiuk. First, for being my *hospitalera* colleague in many *refugios* on the way - Nobody cleans bathrooms like you, Daphne! And I am still thankful for every time she volunteered to work the early shift. And the second thank you for co-authoring, editing, and proof-reading this book. Any remaining typos and grammar mistakes are entirely my fault and not hers!

Another special "Thank You" to the *refugio* and the neighbours in Grañón (La Rioja, Spain) and its parish priest Don José Ignacio Díaz Pérez (now in Logroño). This *refugio* and the people of Grañón taught me, more than anything or anyone else, what it means to be a pilgrim, a *hospitalera,* and how to give hospitality.

And last, but certainly not least, a heartfelt "Thank You" to my husband and co-pilgrim, Rev. Ricky Yates, who, while I was writing this book, did more than his usual share of the housework and thus allowed me more time for writing.

## About the Authors

**Sybille Yates** has not only walked more than 6,000 kilometres / 3,700 miles on European pilgrim routes in Spain, France, Italy, and England, but has also helped as a *hospitalera voluntaria* in more than 20 pilgrim *refugios* on the Way. She helped in Spain to train others for this task and helped to provide continuous further training for them, especially with focus on First Aid, History of the Camino de Santiago, and Spirituality. Additionally, she has hands-on experience of renovating old houses into new pilgrim *refugios* and participated in "pilgrim preparation days" in England. She is, together with her husband Rev. Ricky Yates, a member of the Confraternity of Saint James (Great Britain).


**Daphne Hnatiuk** walked the Camino Francés for the first time in 2003 and was infected with the incurable "Camino bug". Since then she has spent many months over the past 10 years in Spain as both a pilgrim and a *hospitalera voluntaria*. She has walked Camino routes north, south, east, and west in Spain as well as in Southern France and Northern Italy and can often be seen with her camera and pen and paper in hand, updating English language guide books / web pages and taking pictures while walking the Way. In 2008 she walked the Camino Francés a third time to update "Walking the Camino de Santiago, 3rd edition PiliPala Press". She cherishes and thanks all the pilgrims with whom she has shared the Way and feels very privileged that they in turn have shared their hearts and their stories with her. When not on the Camino, Daphne lives in Vancouver, Canada where she keeps her Camino connection alive by editing guidebooks and answering the questions of future pilgrims.

# Appendix

## Customizable Packing List

Once again, here is the download link to the packing list templates on my website:

http://www.caminosantiago.eu/packing-list/

## Emergency Numbers in Spain

In Spain, the central emergency number is **112** as it is throughout Europe. Spanish is obviously the language spoken by all telephone operators, but some are also able to speak English, German, or French, among other languages. So don't be afraid to call when you have an emergency, even if you don't speak (much) Spanish. Chances are good there will be somebody available that speaks a language you do speak.

Since 2012, the Spanish police have had a "foreign language" hotline. This one is not meant for emergencies but rather for reporting minor crimes, like thefts for example. The number is **902 102 112** and is manned from 09:00h to 21:00h. Further information can be found here:

http://www.policia.es/denunweb/den_tel_es.html.

## Free Resources:

An English pilgrim forum has put together a superb PDF file which lists *refugios* on the Way, where to find shops, ATMs, etc. You can download it for free from their website: http://www.caminodesantiago.me/camino-de-santiago-guides/albergues-on-the-camino-frances/

At http://www.godesalco.com/plan you can specify your itinerary and then download several customized files with height profiles, GPS way points, KML files, and a simple guide to the different localities you will pass by. **Extra Tip**: Do not over plan things in the beginning but rather just enter in your start and end point as this will give you far more flexibility later on.

Also http://www.openstreetmap.org/ provides free maps, either to print out or to load into your GPS.

## Addresses of Spanish Tourism Offices abroad

You can find information about travelling in Spain and even download some free information. Instead of writing out an endless list of addresses, here is their central website, where you can find, in English, the address of the one nearest to you. Website: http://www.spain.info/en/

## On-line Outdoor Shops

Some items are simply cheaper and/or easier to order on-line. Here are some on-line shops that have worked well for us over the years. Remember that things that need to "fit like a glove", for example a backpack and shoes, need to be tried on personally before being bought.

http://www.amazon.com
http://www.decathlon.com
http://www.froggtoggs.com/
http://icebreaker.com
http://www.mec.ca/
http://www.anaconda.com.au/
http://www.kathmandu.com.au/
http://rei.com/
http://www.kathmandu.co.nz/
http://www.macpac.co.nz/ (international website of the company with links/redirect to the appropriate website for your country)

## Pilgrim Chariots and handcarts
http://www.chariotderandonnee.com/
http://monowalker.com/
http://www.carrix.ch/

**English Speaking Pilgrims Forum**

http://www.caminodesantiago.me/board

**Find out more about Five Finger Shoes®**
http://www.vibramfivefingers.com

**Anti-Bed Bug Information**

http://bedbugger.com/

**Anti Bed Bug Products**

http://www.sawyer.com/bugs.html

**Sending things you don't need anymore ahead to Santiago de Compostela**

If you have already booked a pension or hotel in Santiago, you can send superfluous items to that address. Don't forget to put your own name c/o Name of Hotel on the parcel and warn the hotel beforehand that they will get a parcel for you. Hotels and pensions will then, normally, keep the parcel until your planned arrival date, especially if you pre-paid your room when booking.

Another possibility is to use the luggage storage service offered by Ivar Rekve, see

http://www.caminodesantiago.me/luggage-storage-in-santiago-de-compostela/

## Addresses of Camino Associations and Confraternities

Here you can apply for your pilgrim passport (*credencial*), take part in pilgrim preparation days, and meet other pilgrims. Please note that the street addresses are often "postal only". Before trying to drop into an association office, check the website for opening hours etc. Most of the associations mentioned below also run pilgrimage related events in locations other than their office address, so if you live in another corner of the country don't hesitate to contact them and ask! If your country is not represented here, the best thing to do is to get in touch with The Confraternity of St. James, London, UK (first address) and asked to be put in contact, if possible, with a member from your home country!

## UK

The Confraternity of St. James
Marion Marples
Secretary, Confraternity of St James
27 Blackfriars Road
London SE1 8NY
United Kingdom
Tel: (+44) (0)20 7928 9988
Fax: (+44) (0)20 7928 2844
Website: http://www.csj.org.uk/

## Ireland

Irish Society of the Friends of St. James
Cumann Cáirde San Séamus i nÉirinn
The Secretary
36, Upper Baggot Street
Dublin 4
Ireland
Tel: (+353) 085 781 9088 - Only Monday - Friday 10.00 - 12.00!
Website: http://www.stjamesirl.com/

**Australia and New Zealand**
Australian Friends of the Camino
P.O. Box 601
Stirling
South Australia 5051
Australia
List of Websites: http://www.csj.org.uk/australia.htm

**United States**
American Pilgrims on the Camino
1514 Channing Avenue
Palo Alto CA 94303-2801
Fax (+1) 650 989 4057
Website: http://www.americanpilgrims.com/

**Canada**
The Canadian Company of Pilgrims
P.O. Box 57004
Ottawa, Ontario
K1R 1A1
Website: http://www.santiago.ca/

**Quebec**
Du Québec à Compostelle
650, rue Girouard Est
Saint-Hyacinthe, (Québec)
J2S 2Y2
Canada
Website: http://www.duquebecacompostelle.org/

**South Africa**

Confraternity of St. James of South Africa

Pam Miller

1 Shiraz, 26 Arum Rd

Bloubergrant, 7441

(+27)  072 247 9047

Website: http://www.csjofsa.za.org/


**Addresses of Spanish Embassies in your country**

Most pilgrims will not need these, but someone who needs to walk with an assistance dog should ask the embassy beforehand what kind of paperwork needs to be completed to get said dog recognized as an assistance dog in Spain. To find the Spanish embassy closest to you, use this website: http://www.maec.es/en/EYC/Paginas/embajadas-consulados.aspx

and click 'Versión texto' to see a full, worldwide listing of them.


**Addresses of your embassies / consulates in Spain**


**United Kingdom**

The UK has several embassies and consulates in Spain, the two in Madrid and Bilbao are the ones that cover the whole of the Camino Francés, the Camino del Norte and part of the others ways. See also their website:

http://ukinspain.fco.gov.uk/en/

for further details.

## Madrid

Torre Espacio

Paseo de la Castellana 259D

28046 Madrid

Tel: 902 109 356 (if calling from within Spain)

Tel: (+34) 91 334 2194 (International/alternative number)

Fax: (+34) 917 146 401

**Bilbao** - The British Vice Consul, Graham Cunningham and his staff are only available by prior appointment, please use the under Madrid mentioned telephone numbers to arrange this.

## Ireland

Besides the embassy in Madrid, there are also 10 honorary consulates throughout the country. Please refer to the embassy's website to find out their contact details.

Ireland House

Paseo de la Castellana 46-4

28046 Madrid

Tel: (+ 34) 91 436 4093 (also for emergencies)

Fax: (+34) 91 435 1677

Website: http://www.embassyofireland.es

## Australia

Torre Espacio

Paseo de la Castellana, 259D - Level 24

28046 MADRID

Tel: (+34) 91 353 6600

Fax: (+34) 91 353 6692

Website: http://www.spain.embassy.gov.au

**New Zealand**

Pinar 7, 3rd floor

Madrid

Tel: (+34) 915 230 226

Fax: (+34) 915 230 171

Website: http://www.nzembassy.com/spain

**United States**

Consular Section

c/ Serrano, 75

28006 Madrid

Tel: (+34) 91 587 2200

Fax: (+34) 91-587-2303

Emergency numbers: (+34) 91 587 2240 or (+34) 91 587 2200 (after hours)

Website: http://madrid.usembassy.gov/

**Canada**

Torre Espacio

Paseo de la Castellana 259D

28046 Madrid, España

Tel: (+34) 91 382 8400

Fax: (+34) 91 382 8490

**South Africa**

Edificio Lista

Calle de Claudio Coello 91-6

Cor of J Ortega Y Gasset

28006 Madrid

Tel: (+34) 91 436 3780

Fax: (+34) 91 577 7414

## *Correos* / Post Office in Santiago de Compostela

The main post office (*correos*) in Santiago de Compostela is at the address below. This address is written in the same format that you have to use when you write your address on a parcel. You need to add in / change the parts in **bold**. Please note that the main post office **only keeps parcels for 15 days!** Some pilgrims have reported that this time will be prolonged if you write "PEREGRINO llegada (arrival) + the date of your approximate arrival" on your parcel but I wouldn't bet on it. Another trick, which was successful for some pilgrims, is to write your name and the address of the main post office in Santiago as the FROM address on your parcel. But what if this doesn't work?

Peregrino/a llegada **date of your approximate arrival**
**First Name LAST NAME**
Lista de Correos
Travesa de Fonseca,
15705 Santiago de Compostela
España

**Some other post office addresses on the Camino in France and Spain**

**St. Jean-Pied-de-Port**
1 rue de la poste
64220 Saint-Jean-Pied-de-Port
Tel : 0559379004
Opening hours: Monday to Friday: 09:00 – 12:00 and 14:00 – 17:00, Saturday: 09:00 to 12:00, Sunday closed
To find other post offices in France, have a look at this website: http://www.laposte.fr

## Pamplona

Paseo Sarasate 9 (Ground Floor)

31002 - Pamplona

Tel: 948-207217 and 902-197197

Fax: 948-222009

Opening hours: Monday to Friday: 08:30 – 20:30, Saturday: 09:30 to 14:00, Sunday closed

## Logroño

Perez Galdos 40

26001 Logroño

Tel: 941286802

Fax: 941209800

Opening hours: Monday to Friday: 08:30 – 20:30, Saturday: 09:30 to 14:00, Sunday closed

## Santo Domingo de la Calzada

Avenida Burgos, 10-12

26250 - Santo Domingo de la Calzada

Tel: 941341493

Fax:941341493

Opening hours: Monday to Friday: 08:30 – 14:30, Saturday: 09:30 to 13:00, Sunday closed

## Burgos

Plaza Conde de Castro 1

09002 Burgos

Tel: 947256597

Fax: 947265711

Opening hours: Monday to Friday: 08:30 – 20:30, Saturday: 09:30 to 14:00, Sunday closed

**Léon**

Jardin de San Francisco 2

24004 Leon

Tel: 987876081

Fax: 987876078

Opening hours: Monday to Friday: 08:30 – 20:30, Saturday: 09:30 to 14:00, Sunday closed

**Astorga**

Correos 3

24700 Astorga

Tel: 987615442

Fax: 987615442

Opening hours: Monday to Friday: 08:30 – 14:30, Saturday: 09:30 to 13:00, Sunday closed

**Ponferrada**

General Vives, 1

24400 Ponferrada

Tel: 987403187

Fax: 987410928

Opening hours: Monday to Friday: 08:30 – 20:30, Saturday: 09:30 to 13:00, Sunday closed

To find other post offices in Spain, have a look at this website: http://www.correos.es/

## Some other useful addresses in Santiago de Compostela

### Oficina de Peregrinos ( Pilgrim's Office)

The Pilgrim's Office is near the cathedral and signposted from all directions. Here pilgrims get their *compostela* and you can get some help in finding accommodation - OK, most of the time you just get a list of addresses.

Rúa do Vilar, 3/1

15705 Santiago de Compostela (A Coruña)

Tel.: +34 981 568 846

Fax: +34 981 563 924

Summer (Easter Monday until the end of October): Monday to Sunday 9:00- 21:00

Winter (November until Easter Sunday) Monday to Sunday 10:00 – 20:00

Lunch break normally between 14:00-16:00 during the quiet season and on Sundays and Feast Days.

Website: http://www.peregrinossantiago.es/

**Text of the** *Compostela*

Original text in Latin

"CAPITULUM hujus Almae Apostolicae et Metropolitanae Ecclesiae Compostellanae sigilli Altaris Beati Jacobi Apostoli custos, ut omnibus Fidelibus et Perigrinis ex toto terrarum Orbe, devotionis affectu vel voti causa, ad limina Apostoli Nostri Hispaniarum Patroni ac Tutelaris SANCTI JACOBI convenientibus, authenticas visitationis litteras expediat, omnibus et singulis praesentes inspecturis, notum facit : (Latin version of name of recipient) Hoc sacratissimum Templum pietatis causa devote visitasse. In quorum fidem praesentes litteras, sigillo ejusdem Sanctae Ecclesiae munitas, ei confero.

Datum Compostellae die {...} mensis {...} anno Dni {...} Canonicus Deputatus pro Peregrinis"


English translation

"The Chapter of this Holy Apostolic Metropolitan Cathedral of Saint James, custodian of the seal of Saint James' Altar, to all faithful and pilgrims who come from everywhere over the world as an act of devotion, under vow or promise to the Apostle's Tomb, our Patron and Protector of Spain, witnesses in the sight of all who read this document, that: Mr/Mrs/Ms {they will insert your name in Latin here} has visited devoutly this Sacred Church in a religious - pious sense. Witness whereof I hand this document over to him, authenticated by the seal of this Sacred Church.

Given in Saint James of Compostela on the {day} ...... {month} ...... A.D. ...... Canon in charge of the Pilgrims Office"


**Text of the** *Certificado*

Here is the Spanish text of the simpler *certificado* given to those pilgrims who declared that they didn't do the pilgrimage for religious nor for spiritual reasons, but rather for cultural or sportive ones.


"La S.A.M.I. Catedral de Santiago de Compostela le expresa su bienvenida cordial a la Tumba Apostólica de Santiago el Mayor; y desea que el Santo Apóstol le conceda, con abundancia, las gracias de la Peregrinación."

English translation

"The Holy Apostolic Metropolitan Cathedral of Santiago de Compostela expresses to you its heartfelt welcome to the Tomb of the Apostle St. James the Greater; and wishes that the holy Apostle may grant you, in abundance, the graces of the Pilgrimage."

## Sample Text for a pilgrim's recommendation letter in Spanish

Con esta carta de recomendación certifica la Parroquia {name of parish} en {place}, {insert your country name in Spanish}, obispado de {diocese}, que {name}, nacido el {date of birth} en {place of birth}, ha sido enviado por esta parroquia como peregrino {a pie = by foot, en bicicleta = on bycicle, en caballo = on horseback} desde {starting point} a Santiago de Compostela.

{date}, {place}

{Name of minister}, Párroco


Translation:

This letter of recommendation certifies the parish of {name of parish} in {place}, {insert your country name in Spanish}, diocese of {name of diocese}, that {your name}, born {date of birth} in {place of birth}, has been sent by this parish as a pilgrim by {a pie = by foot, en bicicleta = on bicycle, en caballo = on horseback} from {starting point} to Santiago de Compostela.

{date}, {place}

{Name of minister}, parish priest

And don't forget to get it stamped with the stamp of the parish / Church!

## Sample Text of a Pilgrim's Blessing

For many hundreds of years, this, or a similar, pilgrim's blessing has been given to pilgrims that pass through Roncesvalles and other Churches of the Way.

The English translation is below, feel free to adapt it to your own needs:

"Almighty God, you who has called your servant Abram out of the Chaldean city of Ur and watched over him during all his travels, you, who were the guide of the Hebrew people in the desert, we ask you to take care of these your children, who, for the love of your name, start their pilgrimage to Santiago de Compostela.

Be for them companion on the way, guide at the crossroads, strength in weariness, defence in danger, shelter on the way, shade in the heat, light in the darkness, comfort in despair and firmness in their intentions.

So that they, with your help, might arrive safely at the end of their journey and enriched by grace and virtues, might return safely to their homes - filled with everlasting joy.

We ask this through Jesus Christ, your Son, who lives and reigns with you in the unity of the Holy Spirit, one God, for ever and ever.

May the blessing of God Almighty, Father, Son and Holy Spirit, be with you and remain with you always. Amen.

Go in the peace of the Lord, who himself is The Way and pray for us in Compostela."

## The Lord's Prayer in Spanish

Those who want to at least pray the Lord's Prayer with the congregation during the mass might find this useful:

*Padre nuestro, que estás en el cielo,*
*santificado sea tu Nombre;*
*venga a nosotros tu reino;*
*hágase tu voluntad en la tierra como en el cielo.*
*Danos hoy nuestro pan de cada día;*
*perdona nuestras ofensas,*
*como también nosotros perdonamos*
*a los que nos ofenden;*
*no nos dejes caer en tentación*
*y líbranos del mal.*
*Amén.*

OK, that really was it! I hope this additional information and the addresses here in the appendix will help you and please remember, if you found this book useful, to review it on Amazon. If you still have questions, you can reach me via my website here: http://www.caminosantiago.eu/kontakt/

# ¡Buen Camino!

DA JAN 1 3 2017 ✔

43959579R00079

Made in the USA
San Bernardino, CA
03 January 2017